# Near Death Experiences Vol. 2

## The Truth Revealed

**Conrad Bauer**

*ISBN: 978-1981359301*

*Printed in the United States*

# **Contents**

# Where Do We Begin?

You're alive now, but you know that won't last forever, and so you have no doubt wondered what might happen when you die. Philosophers and organized religion alike have sought to answer this age-old question ever since man had the temerity to ask it in the first place. Adding fuel to the speculation are the supposed eyewitness accounts of the other side that we refer to as "near-death experiences."

Yes, just as thousands of years ago an Egyptian construction worker might have gotten knocked off his scaffold by a piece of falling pyramid only to report an NDE, there are still people who claim to have seen what lies beyond death's door. Those of us who have considered the "big questions" in life can't help but be intrigued by such narratives.

I can clearly remember the first time I came upon the concept of near-death experiences; it was a real eye-opener. I was 10 years old and had just barely conceived of mortality, but after raiding my older brother's bookshelf for a copy of Raymond A. Moody's classic *Life After Life* (pretty heavy stuff for a 10-year-old, huh?), I was hooked.

Even at that young age, the idea of our consciousness continuing after this life seemed like a powerful and alluring topic. But as I progressed through my reading, I got past the question of what might happen when we die. I began to consider another question: Why are we here at all?

Those are the two main questions religions the world over have attempted to come to grips with for millennia: What happens when we die, and why are we here in the first place? But beyond the "whys" and all the "what happens," as my ten-year-old brain searched for answers, I stumbled upon an even bigger question. Not so much why are we here, but *how* are we here?

I began to think to myself: If we were created by God, then who created God? Where did God come from? How could something just exist with no beginning and end? Suddenly everything seemed impossible. Nothing should exist. There shouldn't be any people, animals, or Earth at all; there should be just a blank page of nothing!

The human mind follows a natural progression, and in our minds it doesn't make sense that something could have no beginning and no end. However, this impossibility is what our limited understanding is forced to accept. Even if you take the concept of God out of the equation and turn to science, science cannot explain this conundrum any better. In fact, it gets worse.

Because if you believe in the theory of the Big Bang, you logically have to ask yourself, where did the Big Bang come from? If all of creation began as one finite molecule that exploded into existence 14 billion years ago, then where did that molecule come from? How did it just spontaneously pop into existence all by itself? Or how could it just exist for all eternity with no beginning or end in sight?

No mother, no father, no creator or parent electron; that molecule just existed, for no apparent reason. As you can see, you end up back at square one. Just as we can't figure out who created God, from the scientific perspective we can't explain where that molecule came from or why the Big Bang went bang in the first place. There are no easy answers to these questions.

This is what is so intriguing about near-death experiences. Those who've had them seem to have been given a glimpse outside of our current understanding of reality, and the priceless gems of information they return with might facilitate a better understanding of these cosmic mysteries. It may not give us all of the answers we seek during our finite human existence, but at least it's a start.

This is my second book on near death experiences (NDE). In the following pages, as it was also included in volume 1, you'll discover what is a NDE, how science explains this phenomenon, a brief history of NDE across the World, the role of Angels, and celebrities that had a NDE. We will then move on to cases of people who had an NDE. If you would like to go directly to the cases, please go to page 33.

# What is a Near Death Experience?

The term "near death experience" can be incredibly evocative. While for some it might simply suggest the proximity to an accident or a personal tragedy, the meaning behind a near death experience is often a great deal more spiritual.

For those who have been involved in a near death experience (or NDE), the event is not just a health or mortal concern. Instead, the process of moving close to the end of life and coming back again is enough to encourage questions of what lies beyond this plane of existence, and what their death means to a wider world. For those who have been unfortunate enough to have an NDE, the process can be traumatic, life affirming, terrifying, and a life-defining moment.

The accounts of those involved in a near death experiences can differ wildly. There are often similarities, but many of the most interesting aspects of the phenomena arise from the slight variations in accounts which are given by those who have approached death and returned back to tell the tale.

Whether a person has been clinically dead or has simply come dangerously close, the rise in modern medicine has certainly increased our ability to save lives. As well as this, however, it has blurred the line between the living and the dead, changing the place at which we might consider a person beyond the pale of existence. For those who have near death experiences, what information, stories, and warnings do they have to tell the rest of the world?

Perhaps the first thing which we should do is to define the near death experience. This can be difficult, with many of the most famous examples differing hugely in the specific details. There are, however, a number of shared aspects and common experiences which can help us to define these events and can help us learn more about what people are experiencing.

The most important attribute is always the life of the person. We label these events "near death experiences" because of their proximity to death. Because there is such a final quality to our lives, the ability to come so close to death and to return will inevitably give these events a more revered quality, especially when compared to the more turgid experiences which we may encounter in our day-to-day lives.

While it might be considered a morbid and taboo subject in many cultures, considerations and thoughts of what happens after death is fascinating for a large amount of the population. Because of this, those who might be able to offer insight and thoughts in this regard are often given platforms to speak. When we want to define the near death experience, our own mortality as humans will always play a large role.

Many people come close to death on a regular basis. As a matter of course, you may be involved with a car accident or trip down the stairs, have a long illness, or even become a victim of violent crime. While these experiences may bring us closer to death, they are not what we might label a near death experience. For this particular label and to understand this particular phenomena, it is important to understand that there is another element involved.

In this respect, many people who look into the cases of NDEs often find that there is an element of the supernatural, the spiritual, the religious, or the just plain strange. It might be sensations of levitation, an out-of-body experience, the sight of angels and/or demons, a feeling of complete serenity, or even just feeling of being warm and comforted. These abstract sensations are what separates the near death experience from simply nearly dying. Rather than a medical procedure, they are spiritually involving. Rather than simply transitioning from one state to another, those who have come back from the edge often tell us of their experiences and how they are so different from everything else they may have undergone before.

As such, there is a desire to investigate and find out more about the near death experience. Because it can be so difficult to quantify and even more difficult to replicate, the investigations into the phenomena are often wild stabs in the dark. For those who are seeking answers, the NDE is unlikely to provide measured explanations. For some people, this makes the stories surrounding near death experiences hard to believe, while for others, it is often what makes them so compelling.

By steering clear of simple and easy answers, we are given a great deal of room for interpretation and reflection. Much in the same way that people can be given the raw facts of a story and reach different interpretations, the near death experience offers listeners, participants, observers, and sceptics equal opportunity to find out more about what is really happening. Unlike most events in a person's life, however, there are very rarely definitive answers. This subjectivity is what fuels a huge amount of interest in the NDE and goes some way to explaining the public's intrigue into what can be both a deeply personal and a deeply subjective experience.

**So how best to define the near death experience?**

The essentials are that a person comes close to dying and in doing so, has an experience of a spiritual nature. It might be that they are declared clinically dead – though this is not essential – and before being revived, they encounter a vision or experience which is unlike anything they have encountered before.

Building on these vital elements are several points that can embellish and flesh out our understanding of what an NDE really means. Bruce Greyson, a researcher who is responsible for much of what we know about these events, describes several broad categories of experiences that are shared by many of those who come close to death.

As suggested by Greyson, there is often a sensation that one is outside of their own body and observing events in the immediate vicinity. This could be a person watching doctors perform surgery on them or seeing first responders cutting them out of a crashed car. There can be visions of deceased or absent relatives, like a grandfather who has passed or a sister who is hundreds of miles away. Greyson also describes the regularity with which typical boundaries are easily broken, whether they are time or space related. It might be that seconds feel like hours or vice versa. It might be that the experience transports a person thousands of miles away or brings their loved ones closer.

While not every experience is the same and while not every experience shares the exact same traits, these features often contribute to what has become commonly regarded as a near death experience. When thinking about NDEs, this is what we typically understand. As we will find out later, however, these experiences can be utterly unique and fascinating.

# History of the Near Death Experience

Unlike many aspects of spirituality and the unknown, the advances made in science and medicine have been able to detect and record more near death experiences, and the volume of public information now available regarding these kinds of events. For researchers, this is down to two main factors:

- The advancements in medical knowledge and procedures
- Our ability to communicate information more effectively

As we have gotten better at treating illnesses and the damage caused by accidents, our ability to revive and heal is greater than ever before. Advances in equipment have meant that our chances of bringing people back from the edge of death are higher than ever before.

On top of this, the widespread use of the internet, 24-hour news channels, and the ready availability of book publishing means that we have a greater ability to tell one another of NDEs more than ever before in human history.

Thanks to the work of historians, we have reports of near death experiences that have been passed down through the centuries. First-hand accounts and primary sources are more difficult to locate due to the vast amount of time that has passed, the lack of literacy, and the limited durable printing materials available. However, texts such as the Bible and the Koran are two of the most enduring books of all time and both hint at instances of NDE.

The first account is even older than either of these texts. The Greek philosopher Plato gives us a description of what sounds remarkably like a near death experience in the tenth book of his famous Republic.

Plato from the school of Athens painted by Raphael in 1509

The reader learns about Er, a soldier who is laid on a funeral pyre and presumed to be dead. Waking up at the last minute, Er tells everyone about his passage into the afterlife. For Plato, the story of Er is more than just an anecdote. The elements of the story were woven into the wider philosophical argument of his book; the light of truth, the journey of the soul as a celestial being, and a great vision of light are all elements which we might recognize today as being similar to many contemporary accounts.

For those looking for exact details in the Bible, there have been many disagreements. For example, a large number of people choose to use 2 Corinthians 12:2-5 as evidence for a biblical NDE. Doing so might seem like interpretation to fit the needs of the interpreter to take liberties with the text, however, working under the assumption that Paul had technically passed away before finding himself in the kingdom of heaven would indeed make it a NDE.

While this is not stated in the text explicitly, many people choose to interpret this event as a near death experience. Whether the event was a vision or a literal experience, the willingness to interpret and investigate the story by people throughout the ages can itself be taken as evidence of an awareness and the need throughout the ages to understand near death experiences.

Another issue with interpreting Biblical passages is the presence and role of Satan in the text. In the Bible, the devil is a deceptive and unreliable character, willing to twist the thinking of those he encounters. For those searching through books such as Corinthians, sceptics have pointed to the role of Satan as being possibly deceptive. If he is able to disguise himself as an angel, then the validity of the near death experience is called into question.

In some respects, the Bible remains close-lipped on the issue. However, wider theological questions raised by both the text and stories about Jesus can help to contribute to a wider understanding of the belief underpinning many people's interpretations of the NDE phenomena. Jesus's many descriptions of the journey to heaven and of the qualities of the soul (Luke 10:25-28, Romans 8:39, and others) can be used to bolster what we know about our ancestors' accounts of these experiences. By gaining a comprehension of their theological beliefs, we can fill in the gaps that missing sources and primary texts have failed to clarify. In much the same way that Plato's accounts tell us about Greek interpretations of the NDE, the Bible helps to show readers a historically Christian perspective on these experiences.

Another interesting avenue of history is medicine. As mentioned above, the growing abilities of physicians means that there is not only a higher chance of patients recovering, but also a wider interest in documenting their experiences. Our oldest medical description of such an event involves a French doctor at the midpoint of the eighteenth century.

Writing in 1740, Pierre-Jean du Monchaux leaves us his memoirs from his time as a military physician stationed in northern France. He wrote a book entitled *Anecdotes de Médecine*, a collection of stories and anecdotes from his time treating patients. During a description of a patient who has a near death experience, he explains that any NDE stems from too much blood flowing to the head, with the brain becoming overrun with a sudden rush after returning to consciousness.

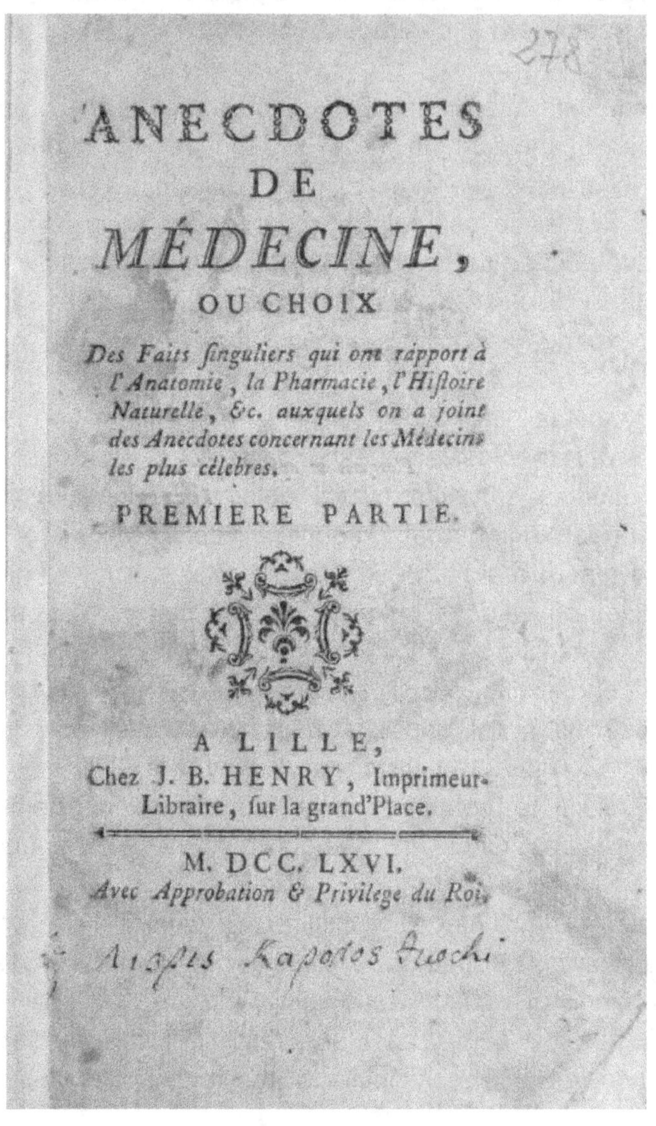

One current figure in the study of the near death experience is another Frenchman. Dr. Philippe Charlier is not only a doctor, but an archaeologist as well. He is well-regarded in his home country as a forensic investigator of historical figures. In the process of general research, Charlier happened across another centuries-old description in a book originally purchased from an antique store.

Speaking to Live Science, Charlier described his interest in the history of medicine and in the practices which have grown and evolved into what we currently know. His particular period of interest is the eighteenth century, which is the timeframe in which his antique store find was written. While not a landmark book by any means, the text did provide interesting reading about the history of the near death experience.

As detailed in the book, a famous pharmacist (an apothecary, as they were known at the time) in Paris fell into a deep unconsciousness. Upon waking, he describes having seen an incredibly pure and bright light which he likens to heaven.

At the time, the lack of understanding or knowledge about the near death experience led to both dismissal and curiosity. The events that we might today view as profound and life changing were back then often misunderstood. As Charlier says, they were more willing to attribute the event to the supernatural.
In other investigations and research, he also reports a variety of vivid and sensational emotions which overcome what we would now describe as near death experiences. The communications with the deceased and the large amount of bright and heavenly light are very similar to the pattern which we are now able to recognize.

Going back to the descriptions of Monchaux, the comparisons with the patient undergoing what was then a strange and bizarre case is comparable and remarkably similar to the events which Charlier has uncovered. When thinking about historical cases of NDE, it might come as a surprise that the French medical community in the 1700s provides so much insight. But with the wars, revolutions and upheaval in the country at the time, cases of hypothermia, drowning, hanging, and other threats to human life should not make the prevalence surprising.

While both Monchaux and the writers of Charlier's documents speculated on the medical reasoning behind the events which they described, their explanations of rushes of blood and trapped veins were, at best, wild speculation. As mentioned above, the increasing level of medical understanding and the increasing need to document all medical oddities and experiences has eventually led to an even greater understanding. That is why we are in perhaps the most interesting position regarding history and the near death experience. Unlike those who are quick to dismiss miracles and other phenomena, advances in technology and medicine have only provided more material for researchers and interested parties to investigate the experiences of those who come so close to death.

# Worldwide Phenomena

If you are in any way interested in the phenomenon of the near death experience, then one fascinating element is the manner in which other cultures have reported similar events. One of the foremost scholars into culture-spanning studies of the subject is Gregory Sushan. In his work, Sushan has examined accounts from five of the most important civilizations in the history of mankind:

- Vedic India
- Old and Middle Kingdom Egypt
- Pre-Buddhist China
- Sumerian and Old Babylonian Mesopotamia
- Pre-Columbian Mesoamerica

Taking these cultures into account, it might surprise people to discover the prevalence of near death experiences, the very similar process of the shamanic afterlife, and the journeys which souls can expect. Across all of the different societies, the nine most prevalent elements of the modern NDE are echoed in events of the past. By examining these similarities, Sushani has been able to support both religious and physiological theories.

For those looking for an overview of all of the anthropological and cultural studies which have been conducted with regards to NDEs and the cultural differences, Augustine's 2003 study is a great place to start. As a conclusion, it is suggested that the actual content of the NDEs does not change by a huge amount. Instead, it is simply the identity of the key figures within the experiences which change. Rather than Jesus, for example, those raised in a Hindu culture might meet

Yamaraja, who is the Hindu king of death. These minor changes indicate the widespread prevalence of the key tenants of the NDE with minor variations.

Published in the Journal of the American Society for Psychical Research in 1986, Satwant Pasricha and Ian Stevenson conducted research which examined the details of sixteen cases of NDE in India. Despite the small sample size, Pasricha and Stevenson were able to draw parallels between Indian and Western NDE events, though there were some differences. While American subjects might report being able to see their own body from a distance, this is not present in Indian accounts. The journey to another world is also slightly different, in that Indian reports would usually include a third party taking the deceased person to an afterlife, at which point it would be discovered a mistake had been made and the subject would wake up. This is slightly different from American accounts, in which a deceased relative will perform this role. The Western patient will often report returning out of love or a sense of unfinished business rather than what appears to be a clerical error.

When trying to ascertain the reasons for differences between Hindu accounts and their typically Western counterparts, the key reason often given is the cultural context. For those in the dramatic and confusing circumstance that a near death experience so often is, the need to impose a context and understanding on unfamiliar circumstances typically draws from culture. We use familiar stories, beliefs and religions to make sense of the nonsensical. By using the cultures which we are most familiar with, those across the world are able to make better sense of their individual situation by making use of what they understand about the afterlife and the journey which it might involve.

As well as Hindu interpretations of the near death experience, Sushani uses the world of the ancient Hebrew writers to help our understanding. In the Jewish religion, the ancient people imagined heaven to be in the form of a three-tiered universe: heaven, Earth, and the underworld. Heaven was exclusively the domain of God and angels, humans would occupy the middle world, and deceased peoples' souls would pass through into the third tier, the underworld "She'ol." As well as the better known story of Daniel, the Hebrew Scriptures also give us the story of Elijah and his ascent towards heaven. The reincarnation of Elijah, as described by Malachi, is taken as one of the signs of the arrival of the Messiah. We can read this "reincarnation" as Elijah being revived or returning from a near death experience, a concept which was not entirely unfamiliar to the ancient sect of Judaism. Those who believe in Hasidic Judaism are invested in a belief in reincarnation, an extension and alternate version of which is also taught in the more mystical Kabbalah.

For contemporary Jewish people, the more orthodox practitioners have taken on board the doctrine of the reincarnation, though the non-orthodox believers accept a more metaphysical version – the immortal soul. Whichever specific sect or variant of Judaism a person believes in, the idea of reincarnation and returning from the dead is a very important and core concept.

Another interesting culture which Sushani takes into account means travelling to East Asia. The Tibetan Book of the Dead can be considered something of an instruction manual, telling readers about the passage from the land of the living to the land of the dead. There is an intermediate phase which lasts 49 days, commencing immediately from the moment of death and transitioning from there into a new bodily frame. While ostensibly a philosophical framework around which the Tibetan Buddhists discuss life and death (rather than being an actual account of experiences), the Book of the Dead is interesting as it demonstrates the interweaving of death rituals of the religion which existed before Buddhism, Bonism. Unlike many religions, the path to death is also the path to life; the process of reviving and reincarnating is intrinsically linked to the religion and the practitioners' beliefs.

And as we look at religions around the world, as well as personal accounts from history, we begin to realize how important the transition between life and death becomes in every religion. Though many people might dismiss the near death experience as simple skepticism, the sheer volume and importance of similar events around the world demands that the phenomena be considered more thoroughly.

# A Scientific Explanation?

As strange and confusing as near death experiences might appear to be, the advances in medical technology and knowledge mean that science is not content to simply observe these phenomena. We now want to find an explanation. In collecting together all of the existing theories and suggested explanations, a 2011 article from Scientific American is a great place to start.

The article begins by addressing much of what is commonly understood about the phenomena – that there are a number of common features to be found in many of the experiences. These include a sense of dying and being dead, a sense that the soul has departed from the body, and that there is a voyage towards a bright light in the direction of a different plane of existence. While these sensations are seemingly mystical, scientists are beginning to posit theories as to why and how they might occur.

It has been established that something close to three percent of the population of the United States has had a near death experience, thanks to the results of a recent Gallup poll. Of those who have an NDE, not all of them are actually in danger of dying, with one study reporting as many as half were not in definite danger. Rather, all of the people in question certainly considered themselves to be under threat. Reported all across the country, with records dating back to ancient Greece and beyond, this prevalence makes clear why scientists would be keen to search for an explanation.

Speaking to the Scientific American, Dean Mobbs – a neuroscientist at the University of Cambridge – provides his explanation for some of these events. He suggests that many of the phenomena which are inherently associated with the near death experience can be explained with an understanding of biology. Mobbs works chiefly with his institution's Medical Research Council Cognition and Brain Sciences Unit, and his research in association with Caroline Watt of the University of Edinburgh has provided a large amount of understanding in this field.

One instance which the research focuses on is the sensation of feeling as though one has died. This sensation is not limited to NDEs, and research has unearthed accounts from patients with conditions such as Cotard (or "walking corpse syndrome") in which the patient holds the delusional belief that they have died. Cases such as these typically occur following traumatic events, which include multiple sclerosis or typhoid, and affect the prefrontal cortex and the parietal cortex regions of the brain. The latter of these affects the attentional processes and the former is relevant in cases which exhibit psychiatric conditions such as schizophrenia. Taken together, they give the sufferer a wholly believable feeling of being dead. Understanding of these conditions is not comprehensive, however, and the mechanism which leads to the symptoms is unknown. Mobbs is able to provide a possible suggestion in that the patients could be attempting to make sense of the traumatic experiences which they have endured, with the brain only able to assume that it has died.

Out of body experiences are another factor of the NDE which receives attention from scientists. A very similar occurrence happens when our sleep patterns are interrupted, especially those which come just before sleeping and just before waking. For example, a condition known as sleep paralysis involves the feeling of being paralyzed while still being awake and aware of the surrounding world. It is reported that as many as 40% of adults have been affected by this condition, and it has been heavily linked with very vivid, dream-like hallucinations. These hallucinations can lead to the victim feeling as though they are outside of their own bodies and seemingly floating. In 2005, a study was able to demonstrate that these kind of experiences outside of the body can be artificially induced by triggering or stimulating the right temporoparietal junction in a patient's brain. This would suggest to researchers that confusion over sensory information during an NDE can massively change the way in which a patient interprets the outside world. As with the above research, however, scientists were unable to offer specific information regarding near death experiences or to completely ensure the existence of a link between the conditions.

There have been a variety of suggestions for those who are wondering about the instances of NDE patients supposedly meeting deceased relatives. One comparison which is drawn is the propensity for Parkinson's patients to report visions of people, ghosts, and other such beings while suffering from the condition. The explanation for this is that these patients display an abnormal functioning of dopamine. This means that a neurotransmitter in the brain is capable of evoking such hallucinations in patients.

Similarly, with regard to those who have reported reliving events from their lives or re-enacting memories, one suggestion which scientists have provided concerns the locus coeruleus. This is a midbrain region which is responsible for the release of noradrenaline, a stress hormone which would normally be released while the patient is experiencing high amounts of trauma. The locus coeruleus is one of the brain regions which is highly linked to the mediation of emotion and memory in the mind, with examples including the amygdala and hypothalamus. Near death experiences, it is suggested, can have their symptoms traced to a similar neurological release.

An effect which can be replicated with the use of medicine and even recreational drugs is the general feeling of euphoria which tends to overcome those involved in an NDE. These investigations into chemically reproduced effects include those induced by anesthetic ketamine, a drug which has also been known to trigger hallucinatory experiences and experiences similar to the out-of-body events which are described by so many people.

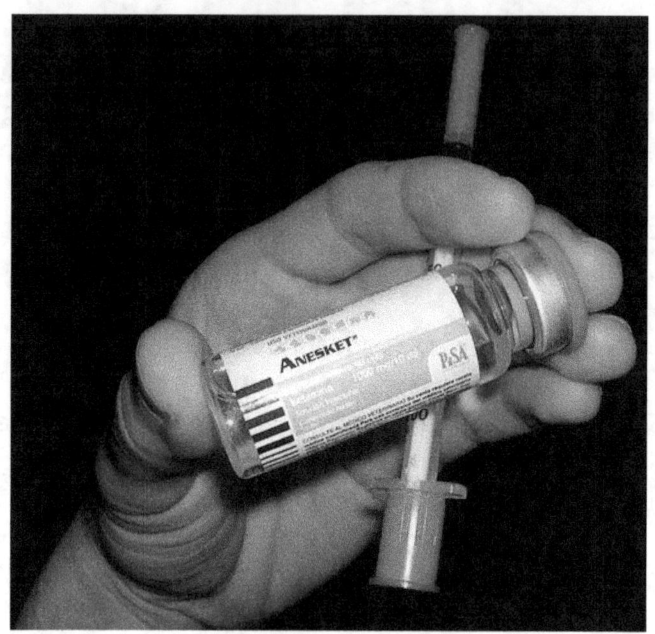

Ketamine, an injectable drug that have similar effects reported in NDE

This is accomplished by affecting the brain's opioid system, a system which can even become active without the use of drugs. Animals who come under attack have had similar events measured, again suggesting that trauma might be the key to triggering a chain of these possible scientific suggestions.

One of the most notorious aspects of the near death experience which has been addressed in Scientific American Magazine is the inclination for those undergoing a near death experience to feel they are heading towards a bright white light. Although the scientists are unable to provide an exact suggestion for these circumstances, there are suggestions that the tunnel vision which can accompany the inhibition of blood and oxygen could resemble a bright light before the eyes. For those suffering from an extreme case of fear or a particular loss of oxygen, this effect could be relevant.

Collectively, one scientific suggestion which is provided for the collection of effects which the body undergoes during an NDE has its basis in the events which occur when normal brain function goes awry. On top of this, the very fact that people are aware of the phenomena has acted as a cultural preparation device which encourages people to know what to expect should they have a brush with death, in effect, a self-fulfilling prophecy.

As per Mobb's suggestions, these findings "provide scientific evidence for something that has always been in the realm of paranormality." This combination of chemical and medical phenomena which could potentially occur all at once might provide us with a template for what happens to the body when it approaches death.

With the wide variety of suggestions which have been made and compared with the wide variety of reports and anecdotes from many people, reaching a conclusion on the exact scientific nature of the near death experience is more difficult than ever. Rather than providing an explanation as to why, medicine has helped us outline the what; that is to say, what happens to the body during a brush with death. Figuring out the exact process will be the next step.

# The Role of Angels

When thinking about the accounts of those who have undergone a near death experience, one recurring factor is the prominence of angels in almost every account. As we will see later in this book, accounts range from the more abstract tales of bright lights to classic depictions of angels as you might find them on the roof of the Sistine Chapel.

Ascent of the Blessed painted in 1490 by Hieronymus Bosh
This painting if frequently  associated by NDE researchers with aspects of the NDE,
namely being transported angels and the tunnel

So, what do we mean by angels? Well, it can help to understand that while typically thought of as an exclusively Christian belief, similar beings exist in many religions. In both Zoroastrianism and Abrahamic religions, these figures are often described as gracious and benevolent beings who are able to act as intermediaries between earth and the afterlife or even as guardian figures who watch over believers.

Their roles have also included protecting humanity, and in the wider Christian canon (books such as Paradise Lost), they have battled against the forces of evil, such as demons. Some angels are given tasks and roles to perform by a divine authority, while others are depicted as innocent cherubs strumming harps while sitting on a cloud. Whatever variety of angel you might be able to imagine, it is sure that someone, somewhere has encountered them during a near death experience.

Because of their almost ubiquitous role in Western religions and their parallel roles in many Eastern religions, it should be no surprise that sightings and encounters with angels have been documented throughout history. A poll which was conducted by Time magazine placed belief in angels among Americans at 69%, while 46% believed that they had a personal guardian angel watching over them. A similar poll by Gallup suggested that 13% of Americans believed that they had encountered an angel or a similar supernatural being.

While the volume of belief in angels among modern day Americans and the similar beings which exist in other cultures and religions does not give us any definitive proof of near death experience accounts, it does help us to understand the belief of people who encounter celestial beings during such events. The facts that the belief is so widespread and the understanding of the role of angels is so apparent give us perhaps more clarity as to why so many people are able to interpret everything from bright lights to robed figures as the same type of being.

Because of the widespread belief in angels and the flexible understanding and interpretation of exactly what they are, the presence of angels in many NDE accounts should come as no surprise.

# Celebrities' Near Death Experiences

Before we examine the near death experiences of various people, it can help to look through several instances of celebrities who have a story to tell. Unlike those who have become famous because of an NDE, these already-famous people bring a slightly different perspective to events.

The rock star Ozzy Osbourne might seem an unlikely candidate for an NDE.

Ozzie Osbourne

However, the English rocker "died twice" following a motorcycle accident which put him into a coma for eight days. After slipping on leaves and being catapulted over the handle bars, the bike fell on top of him and crushed his chest. While his bodyguard tried to help, providing CPR and other immediate care, Ozzy stopped breathing twice. After waking from his coma, Osbourne described his experience as incredibly confusing. At points, he had no idea who he was or where he was. He can distinctly recall a bright light which emerged from the darkness.

While he impresses upon people that he heard "no one blowing trumpets and no man with a white beard," Ozzy's experience is very much in line with other abstract accounts. For someone who was famed for his drug and alcohol consumption, Osbourne used his biography to talk about how these events finally forced him to come to terms with his life and to "grow up."

A name more familiar to older readers might be Jane Seymour. The actress who starred in television show "Dr Quinn, Medicine Woman" and films such as *Somewhere in Time* opposite Christopher Reeves, was 36 years old when she had her near death experience. Jane contracted a very severe bout of flu. To help with the healing process, she was given an injection of penicillin by her doctor. Unfortunately, the actress was quite allergic to penicillin and this only made her illness worse, bad enough to bring her close to death.

Jane Seymour

Seymour describes the experience as she "literally left [her] body." She narrates the sensation of being able to look around the room, to see herself lying in bed and watch as doctors tried to resuscitate her. Moving to the top corner of the room, she floated above them and watched as the medical staff pinned her body to the bed. As they pushed needles into her arms, they had to hold her tightly.

As well as this, she can remember her life "flashing before [her] eyes". Having lived an eventful life, she mentions not thinking about Emmys or awards, but rather being determined to remain alive and return to raise her children. Finally, she began to reason with God, saying, "If you're there, God, if you really exist, and I survive, I will never take your name in vain again." Jane Seymour died for approximately 30 seconds, as she recalls, but suddenly found herself back in her body and woke up.

Another actress who remembers coming close to death is Sharon Stone. The star of *Basic Instinct*, Stone has told of how a brain scare caused her to encounter a bright white light. An artery at the base of her skull was torn by a bad case of internal bleeding. She spoke to Katie Couric about her experience and the journey it put her upon:

Sharon Stone

30

"When it hit me," Stone recalls, "I felt like I'd been shot in the head. That's the only way I can really describe it." The medical emergency is what started Stone along what she described as "a real journey … that took me to places both here and beyond that affected me so profoundly that my life will never be the same … I get to be not afraid of dying, and I get to tell other people that it's a fabulous thing and that death is a gift. And not that you should kill yourself, but that when death comes to you, as it will, that it's a glorious and beautiful thing. This kind of giant vortex of white light was upon me and I kind of - poof! Sort of took off into this glorious, bright, bright, bright white light and I started to see and be met by some of my friends."

And as quickly as it began, Sharon found herself back in the room. While she might not have had the need to turn her life around quite like Ozzy Osbourne, she has spoken about the event as being an incredibly meaningful and important moment in her life.

Perhaps one of the closest examples of a Hollywood star having a life changing near death experience is the story of Gary Busey. Once regarded as one of Hollywood's most notorious party animals and a person who could be considered out of control, Gary Busey was known for his ongoing battles with drugs and drink, eventually leading his wife to dub him "Gary Abusey".

Garey Busey

However, Gary had supernatural and life changing experiences as many as three times during his life. He approached death three times; one a drug overdose, one after contracting cancer, and most pertinently of all, a motorcycle accident that happened in New Mexico. Gary was riding through Albuquerque in 1988 without wearing a helmet. The bike slipped and Busey was thrown headfirst into a roadside curb. Rushed to hospital and placed upon the operating table, Busey recalls a near death experience as doctors fought to save his life.

During this experience, he can recall being surrounded by angels. Rather than the classic versions which might adorn Christmas cards, Busey tells biographers of the angels being simply big balls of light that carried with them nothing but warmth and love of an unconditional nature. After recovering from the accident, Busey remembered his experience near death. He chose to dedicate his life to Jesus and has since become a prominent speaker at many Christian rallies and events. Rather than his addiction riddled past, Gary Busey's NDE has reformed him into a God-fearing man.

# Dr. Eben Alexander Becomes a Believer

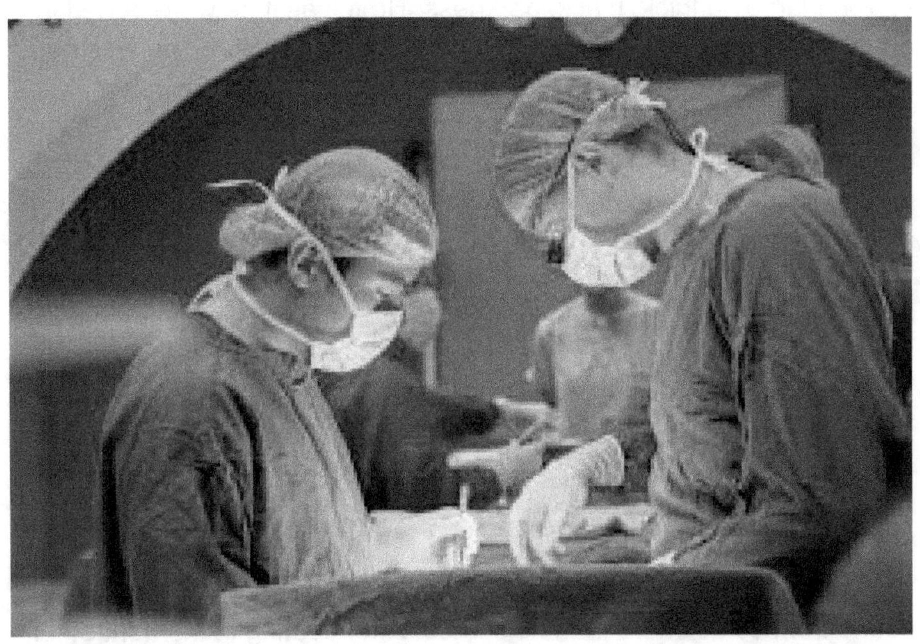

Dr. Eben Alexander was a straight-laced, no-nonsense neurosurgeon who had long believed that stories of NDEs were nothing more than fanciful imagination or the product of a dying mind. That is, until it happened to him! It all began in early November, 2008, when Dr. Alexander became bedridden with what he at first believed to be the flu.

But when he woke up on November 10th, he felt excruciating pain shooting up and down his spine. He could barely function. After a failed attempt to take a bath, he had to drag himself back to his bed, where he eventually erupted into a full blown "grand mal" seizure. His wife walked in on him while he was flailing about and immediately called for an ambulance.

When tests of his cerebrospinal fluid were conducted in the ER it was determined that Dr. Alexander had a severe case of spinal meningitis. His condition rapidly deteriorated, and as he lay writhing in a hospital bed as technicians continued to run tests, he suddenly let out an ear-piercing scream: "God, help me!"

The next thing Dr. Alexander could consciously recall was being surrounded by a thick, black, darkness. He felt as if he were buried in an inky dark blackness of nonexistence. And in this state, he was no longer Eben Alexander. In fact, he didn't even know who Eben Alexander was. As hard as it may be to understand, according to Dr. Alexander, in this form of consciousness he had no name, no personal identity, no family, and none of any of the other trappings that we associate with being alive.

Yet, in some form, Dr. Alexander knew he existed. It was just a dull, empty eternal existence with no point of reference other than the empty blackness that swirled about him for all eternity. It seemed that this vague awareness that he had was all that reality was, or ever would be. There was no one else, just his never-ending stream of dull awareness.

His perfect solitude was eventually interrupted by a dull pounding sound from somewhere in the distance. After floating in the dark ether for what seemed to be an eternity (many NDEs take place outside the normal constraints of time and space), something else had emerged. Dr. Alexander instantly went from being the only thing in the universe to being a witness to this mysterious sound. It was so deep that it was more like a vibration pulsating throughout all creation. It was beating almost like a heart.

And playing right into this imagery, in the darkness that he was immersed in, Dr. Alexander began to see what appeared to be blood vessels in what now seemed to him like a "vast, muddy womb." It is interesting that Dr. Alexander would make this observation, because some near-death experience detractors have offered the theory that in our death throes our mind goes back to the furthest reaches of our memory—often with us winding up with recollections of being in our mother's womb!

Besides those who take this stance, there are also proponents of reincarnation who believe that what Dr. Alexander described is a real experience—but it is not so much a near-death experience as it is a near-birth experience! According to these theorists, someone like Dr. Alexander, who is caught between this life and the next, is in the process of being reborn. What they later recall as an NDE is actually a recollection of literally being reformed in someone's womb.

According to the reincarnation theory, when the spirit ends up going back to their old dying body, this process of rebirth is negated. The woman whose "muddy womb" they were on the verge of reincarnating into suffers a spontaneous miscarriage as a result. It is rather incredible to think that as a heart attack patient is being shocked back to life in the emergency room, the potential new mother his spirit was reincarnating into is having a miscarriage on the other side of the planet!

But these wild theories aside, the "muddy womb" was not the only thing that Dr. Eben Alexander experienced during his trip to the other side. There was much more to come. According to Dr. Alexander, the imagery of his NDE soon began to change. Strange, animalistic faces briefly emerged from the muddy blackness he was immersed in. As terrifyingly odd as this would have been under normal circumstances, in his new state of awareness Dr. Alexander was at first mostly indifferent to the whole thing.

But as he seemed to progress across this strange landscape, he became more uncomfortable. He soon began to feel as if he didn't belong in this strange "muddy womb" at all. He felt as if he were something altogether different from the primordial muck he was encased in. And with this feeling, he finally began to shake off his previous feelings of infinite oneness and once again take on the trappings of a human individual.

As his perception of himself as an individual entity separate from the void began to return, he suddenly felt terrified of being trapped in the darkness he was in. He began to struggle to get out of it. And then, at the nadir of his panicked, despairing attempts to escape from this outer darkness, Dr. Alexander became aware of a new presence in the void. This one was the complete opposite of the dead darkness; this being was "living light."

Dr. Alexander found it difficult to describe this being, but said that it was basically a living ball of energy that radiated "fine filaments of white gold light." Dr. Alexander describes this orb of light slowly spinning as it drew near him. Upon closer inspection, he was amazed that he was suddenly not just looking "at the light" but "through it." The next thing Dr. Alexander knew, there was a flash and "whoosh" of energy and he was instantaneously drawn through this now spinning "vortex" of light.

Light matrices such as this, whether they appear as balls, vortices, tunnels, or literal stairways to heaven, are often perceived in NDEs as a means of transference out of the darkness and into the "light" of a whole new reality. And like so many have stated before him, for Eben Alexander, the new reality that the spinning ball of light transported him to was absolutely breathtaking.

According to Dr. Alexander, after popping out the other side of the portal of light that had sucked him up out of the darkness, he found himself floating through the air, through the atmosphere of a whole new planet. This world was stunningly beautiful, and he could clearly see greenish vegetation, blue waters, and majestic mountains down on the surface. Wherever he was, he knew that it wasn't Earth, yet for some strange reason he felt like he knew the landscape, as if he had been there several times before a long time ago.

This is actually another fairly common theme in NDEs. There are several reports of NDErs emerging into new landscapes only to suddenly realize that they seem oddly familiar. And not just familiar; many who experience this phenomenon have an unshakable and overwhelming feeling that they have just returned "home." As Dr. Alexander recalls, "something pulls at you, and you realize that a part of yourself—deep down—does remember the place after all, and is rejoicing at being back there again."

It is also interesting to note that although Dr. Alexander describes hurtling through the air over this world at an incredible height, his senses had been expanded so much beyond the normal human capacity that he could see even the most minor of details down on the surface. As Dr. Alexander describes it, "I was flying, passing over trees and fields, streams and waterfalls, and here and there, people. There were children too, laughing and playing. The people sang and danced around in circles, and sometimes I'd see a dog, running and jumping among them, as full of joy as the people were." If this man was as high as he says, only an incredible enhancement of the senses could explain how he could spot a dog (and its happy demeanor) jumping and playing on the ground far below him.

After flying around this world, completely content just to observe all the happenings on the surface below for what seemed like a small eternity (he was apparently still outside time as we know it), Dr. Alexander suddenly became aware of another entity sharing his journey with him.

In fact, it was floating right alongside him. This being had a message for him that may seem rather simplistic to many of us. For Dr. Alexander, however, it was the most profound thing he had ever heard. The being instructed him, "You are loved and cherished, dearly, forever. You have nothing to fear. There is nothing you can do wrong." This too is a theme that many NDErs have described. It often comes as a great relief to people who have felt endlessly scrutinized and critiqued in their Earthly existence to discover that there is no judgment in the afterlife.

There's none of the carrot and stick treatment we so often get on this planet, where we're rewarded for our good deeds and smacked over the head for perceived mistakes. Those who've had this type of NDE claim that they experienced a kind of unconditional love that they had never known before. Like a parent who loves their child no matter what, in this afterlife it is made clear that—just as this entity supposedly informed Dr. Alexander—they have "nothing to fear" and that there is nothing they could "do wrong."

The overarching theme is that no matter what happens, you are accepted and loved unconditionally and nothing will change that. Just like a parent loves their child just as much when they fail as when they succeed, this higher love experienced in the afterlife is apparently in it for the long haul as well. This experience, of course, differs from many of the motifs found in Christianity and other religions in regard to specific judgments on the souls of the deceased.

However, as we will see as we progress through this book, some people have NDEs that are far different from the "unconditional love" variety. For some, the scrutiny and judgment they feel in the afterworld is hellish to the extreme. But as for Dr. Eben Alexander, this unconditional love-fest was the overall feeling that he was subjected to. And with this realization of his unconditional acceptance, Dr. Alexander joyfully continued his ascent through the clouds, reveling in the love and sheer happiness he felt.

In the midst of this reverie he noticed several balls of light, which he immediately knew were living entities sojourning through the heavens just as he was. Dr. Alexander, of course, didn't have a mirror on him at the time—but if he did, would he have seen a similar orb reflecting back? Was Dr. Alexander one of these translucent balls of energy bouncing around unobserved for eons in the atmosphere of a strange new world? He was soon going to get his answer.

As he continued his flight, it was as if some higher power had suddenly raised the vibratory level of that reality. It felt as if the very fabric of it had been peeled away, like someone pulling back a curtain. Dr. Alexander found himself in a brightly lit empty space. In this place outside of space and time, he immediately sensed a being of immense power, and he wasted no time in asking, "Where is this place? Who am I? Why am I here?"

Dr. Alexander claims that all of his questions were instantaneously answered in what he could only describe as a massive burst of energy. Exploding all at once, it passed right through him "like a crashing wave" of understanding. There were no words in these replies. Words were not necessary; instead, it was as if the knowledge he sought was downloaded directly into his being upon demand. Dr. Alexander claims that during this exchange he was given knowledge of things so complex that in the normal Earthly approach to learning it would have taken him a lifetime just to understand them.

But somehow, with this direct link-up to this divine being that was live-streaming the data right into his consciousness, he knew and understood the most complex secrets of the universe instantaneously. Dr. Alexander then saw the source of this knowledge. A giant glowing orb emerged in front of him—and he immediately realized that this orb was "God." In his communion with the creator, Dr. Alexander learned that there are several universes, or as he was told, more than he could even conceive of.

It was also revealed that human beings are not the only sentient entities on the block. Yes, that's right, this creator made it clear that what we would term as "aliens" do in fact exist, and he was the one who created them. Just like he created us, he created all of the so-called extraterrestrials as well. Dr. Alexander was even given the privilege of sating his curiosity by being shown overviews of countless worlds scattered throughout the universe inhabited by intelligent alien life. Some of them, he claims, were obviously, "advanced far beyond humanity."

Dr. Alexander's wild ride with the creator of the universe continued as he was taken to even higher dimensions of existence outside of the physical plane. Interestingly enough, although Dr. Alexander claims that all of the revelations he was given are still locked within him, unforgotten, he asserts that now that he is back in this reality, with the limited processing power of a human brain, he is unable to describe most of them, except in the simplest of terms.

According to Dr. Alexander, the human brain just doesn't have the horsepower to handle such data. There is one young woman who had a very similar experience with her own NDE. Just like Dr. Alexander, she had a communion with the creator in which all the secrets of the universe were revealed. But as she described it, as soon as she was sent back into her body and her consciousness was streamed once again through the limited confines of the human brain, it felt as if she was attempting to shove a super computer into a pocket calculator. As a result, most of the knowledge she had gained was impossible to process or explain upon her return.

Skeptics might say that this is a convenient excuse for not being able to back up bold claims, but this concept of the sloughing off of supreme knowledge upon the return to the limited state of the physical body is quite common. Several NDE accounts report this phenomenon. Dr. Alexander himself came to view the human brain as a kind of radio receiver with a "filter" mechanism attached to it.

As our true consciousness is being beamed to the brain from eternity, like a radio signal to a receiver, our extrasensory perceptions are simultaneously being blocked and filtered out. It seems that we are allowed to have just a very narrow bandwidth of existence while here in these mortal shells. Whatever it was that happened to the previously skeptical Dr. Alexander, one thing is for certain: Even now that he's back in the so-called "filter" of everyday life, his outlook will never be the same again.

# Messiah's Near Death Encounter with Satan

Messiah Johnson didn't know how to swim, and this lack of knowledge cost him his life when he slipped and fell into a pool. But drowning was the least of his worries, as he woke up in a strange realm right at the feet of Satan himself!

Messiah had just moved back to his home state of Minnesota to reconnect with the mother of his child, a young woman named Someka. His son was out of school for spring break, and at the time of his dad's visit, he and his little friends were entertaining themselves with a pool party at Someka's apartment complex. Someka had some errands to attend to, and so Messiah offered to watch the kids. She left the apartment, but not before giving him some parting advice: "Don't go swimming. You don't know how to swim." Messiah knew this as well, and he wasn't planning on taking a swim that day. He wasn't even planning on going into the water at all.

But fate would intervene regardless of any plans he had in the matter. His troubles began innocently enough, when a group of kids were happily playing by the side of the pool. Among this group, Messiah noticed that his little niece Kierra was getting dangerously close to the deep end. The kids were playing on a slip and slide, and Messiah feared that she was about to slip off right into the pool and drown.

And after a few moments his fear became reality as she slipped over the edge. Even though she couldn't swim, the quick-thinking child managed to grab hold of the ladder at the deep end and pull herself out of the water. Nevertheless, Messiah was mobilized to action. He immediately went over to pick her out of the pool. He would need more rescuing than she did, however, because as soon as he rushed over to the deep end, he slipped and fell over the edge and into the pool himself.

But unlike his resourceful little niece who managed to land right on the ladder, Messiah fell in such a way that he hit his head on the edge of the pool before plummeting into the water. He was briefly knocked out, and his body sunk down to the bottom of the pool. He remembers coming to a few seconds later as his lungs began to fill with water. He immediately began to panic at the realization that he was drowning. In his distress, all he could see were giant bubbles of air floating up from his submerged form to the surface of the water.

He momentarily struggled to get to the surface, but due to his head injury and the rapid loss of oxygen, he passed out once again. The children on the deck of the pool didn't quite get the gravity of the situation. They were still blithely playing amongst themselves when Messiah's brother Leon came upon the scene. He asked the kids where Messiah was, and they all pointed to the pool. Leon was horrified to see the limp, apparently lifeless body of his brother sprawled out on the bottom.

Unfortunately, Leon wasn't able to swim any better than his brother. Unable to help the dying man directly, he started yelling for others to come to his aid. He managed to gain the attention of some passersby, and they pulled Messiah out of the water and begin to give him CPR. By this point, however, Messiah's vital signs were exceedingly weak and he had taken a lot of water into his lungs. Someone had dialed 911, and an ambulance arrived within minutes. Messiah was loaded inside.

As the emergency vehicle sped off, Messiah coughed up the water his lungs had been holding. Then he completely blacked out. The next thing he knew—much like in the case of Dr. Eben Alexander—Messiah found himself in complete and abject darkness. It was a darkness that could not be seen through and could not be penetrated. From the midst of this darkness he began to hear voices. Strangely, some of the voices began to sound familiar, and they spoke to him as if they knew him and were attempting to give him some small sense of comfort.

The voices told him things like, "It's okay. You'll be alright. Don't be afraid." According to Messiah, after he heard this he quickly realized that he was no longer alive. He intuitively knew that he was dead. Upon this realization, Messiah was filled with questions for the unseen forces pulling and tugging at him. He attempted to engage them in conversation, but the voices would not respond directly to any of his inquiries; they just kept repeating the same catch phrases. "Don't be afraid. You'll be okay."

Growing more and more frustrated, Messiah eventually snapped back, "How am I supposed to believe that everything's okay when you won't even answer my f—g questions?!?" This is perhaps not the best of ways to respond when you are being led over into the afterlife, but Messiah was extremely alarmed from the very beginning. Some NDE researchers have developed the theory that our state of mind when an NDE begins has a lot to do with what manifests and what we ultimately end up experiencing.

If this theory is correct, perhaps it was Messiah's agitated and panicked state of mind that led to the hellish visions that followed. Because according to Messiah, as he was pulled by the unseen force through the darkness, he was taken toward a bright flame that emerged in the distance. As he got closer, he realized that this flame was nothing less than hellfire. Horrified at the thought of being dragged into hell, Messiah screamed and tried with all his might to somehow change his course. But his trajectory was out of his control, and despite all his protests, his push toward the fire continued.

Soon a giant bonfire took shape in the center of the hellish landscape. Right in the middle of it was a pile of what looked like gold coins, and upon this pile of gold coins stood a frightening 12-foot-tall entity with horns on its head and a blood-red face with an extremely intimidating expression. According to Messiah, just as he instinctively knew that he was heading to hell, he also intuitively understood that he was now face to face with the devil himself. Understandably, the thought filled him with absolute terror.

Messiah later related his despair in that moment. He had thought that he was a fairly good person and had tried for the most part to do right in his life. After all, he had drowned in the pool in the selfless act of trying to save his niece! Messiah didn't quite understand why he was in hell, but something told him that he just had to face the facts. And even in the midst of this frightening encounter, he still kept hearing some of the voices telling him to relax and that everything was going to be okay.

Was this some sort of trick to lure him to Satan? Was it just some sort of demonic banter to make him let down his guard and lead him astray? But as Messiah continued to listen, he could clearly recognize one of the voices. It sounded just like his deceased grandmother telling him with firm intensity, "Don't worry! Everything is going to be just fine!" But even as she gave him these words of reassurance, absolute panic and fear gripped Messiah's soul as Satan seemed look in his direction.

It seemed as if he was trying to figure out just who the voices were talking to. (Just leave it to Grandma to call you out like that!) As he stared off into the distance that separated them, the devil finally spotted Messiah and looked him right in the eye. According to Messiah, the devil then simply frowned and looked away. Messiah got the impression—whether telepathically or intuitively—that Satan had decided to "pass on him" for now and focus his attention elsewhere. Even though Messiah was in hell, he was apparently safe for the moment.

After his encounter with Satan was averted, his grandmother's voice piped back in triumphantly. "You see? I told you it would be alright!" (Thanks, Grandma!) It was right at this very moment that the paramedics managed to shock Messiah back to life. The next thing he knew he was out of hell, alive again, and staring up at the roof of the ambulance.

But after his recovery, Messiah couldn't quite shake the hellish vision out of his head. Was this some kind of warning? What did it all mean? Messiah still doesn't have all the answers, but he has since married Someka, the formerly estranged mother of his child, and has done his best to live an exemplary life, in the hopes that he never has to pay Satan a visit ever again!

# Thomas Benedict's Incredible Journey through the Life/Death Barrier

In one of the most incredible and detailed NDEs on record, Thomas Benedict was fully lucid and full of questions. This NDE has a man of great curiosity confronting his creator with the deepest of philosophical inquiries as he travels through the life/death barrier and beyond. His journey to the other side began in 1982, when—for all intents and purposes—Thomas Benedict died of terminal cancer. The cancer was chemo-resistant, and surgery wasn't an option.

He had been informed that he had only about six months to live and advised to make the most of it. His last day on Earth occurred when he woke up in pain at 4:30 AM with an instinctive knowledge that his time had grown exceedingly short. He called up those closest to him to say goodbye one last time, and as his home hospice worker sought to make him as comfortable as possible, he fell into a deep sleep.

The next thing he can consciously recall is stepping right out of his lifeless body and turning back around to see it still lying on the bed. The next thing he realized was that his normal perception was greatly expanded outside of his body. Standing there in spirit form, he could see every part of the house he was in all at once, from the very top of the roof down into the basement.

As he searched every crevice, Thomas noticed a bright source of light in the distance. Facing the source of the illumination, Thomas was instantly drawn to this point of light. It was like magnetism; he couldn't help but go near it. As previously noted, this seems to be a common experience among NDErs. Once they see this physical manifestation of light, it seems to somehow lock onto them—whatever "them" may be at this point—and suck them right up.

Just as a black hole in outer space sucks up everything in its path, this "light hole" is a portal that sucks up spirits! And so it was that Thomas Benedict was being rapidly drawn into this light as well. But in a rare bit of clarity as far as NDEs go, Thomas had the presence of mind to request a slight detour in this journey to the light. He cried out, "Please wait a minute! Just hold on a second here! I want to think about this; I would like to talk to you before I go!"

After he submitted this request to the eternal, to his amazement eternity responded by immediately freezing his NDE in its tracks! An omniscient being of light that Thomas understood to be God then came out of the void and granted him a personal audience. Thomas made it clear early in their conversation that he still had many questions that needed to be answered, and the creator graciously agreed to his request and proceeded to take Mr. Thomas Benedict on what would amount to a grand tour of the universe.

The first leg of this journey was to show him the Earth as it appeared from the spiritual plane. According to Thomas, this was one of the most beautiful things he had ever seen. As he watched the Earth spin on its axis, it was not only a physical mass of rock, water, and air; he could now see what he described as a "mandala of human souls" all growing out of the Earth's fixed position in space and time. For Thomas Benedict, an avowed environmentalist and a bitter cynic when it came to the job humans were doing to take care of the planet, this was an eye opening moment.

Thomas had previously viewed humanity as nothing better than a bunch of parasites, polluting and leaching all the life out of the Earth. But as soon as he saw things how for they really are, he instantly changed his mind. He was made aware of just how special and precious every human soul is. Now, rather than hugging a tree, Thomas suddenly wanted to hug all of humanity! He found himself exclaiming, "Oh, God, I did not know how beautiful we are!"

Thomas realized that every single person on the planet—no matter their actions or behavior while alive—has a soul which is without a doubt the most beautiful thing in all of creation. Thomas maintains that he discovered that the human soul is quite literally a diamond in the rough, the most precious thing in the universe. (Maybe this is why so many horror movies have evil entities trying to steal our souls from us? Because they are just so darn valuable? Just a thought!)

After this revelation, Thomas was transported to another state of existence, in which he saw a giant stream of liquid—shining like light, flowing like water. He asked the creator what this manifestation was, and the creator responded, "This is the river of life; drink of this water to your heart's content." Thomas took these instructions to heart and began drinking and absorbing the "light water" that flowed right in front of him. It is interesting to note that the Christian Bible also has the concept of a "river of life," with Jesus referencing it on many occasions.

So it is intriguing that Thomas Benedict, who was a lifelong atheist, would experience such things in his NDE. For those who argue that near-death experiences are nothing more than the dying brain creating imagery—wouldn't you think that an atheist's dying brain would create something a little more compatible with his belief system? But Thomas Benedict, the former atheist, was more than happy to wade in these spiritual waters.

After fueling up and recharging his being on the cosmic energy emanating from the river of life, Thomas was propelled forward faster than the speed of light as his tour of the universe began in earnest. He saw the Earth hurtling rapidly away from him; then the entire solar system got smaller and smaller as he rocketed off to parts unknown. According to Thomas's extraordinary claims, he was then—in whatever form he may have been in, whether sprit, body, being of light, etc.—he was then sent crashing right into the center of the galaxy.

He contends that as he reached the center of the galaxy it was like he experienced an immense data dump of information. All of the deepest and most profound questions he had ever had were instantly answered. As in Dr. Alexander's experience, one thing that was immediately made clear to Thomas as he acquired this cosmic data was that we are not alone in the universe.

Thomas was made aware that the universe is inherently alive; all of creation is absolutely bristling with life of all kinds, and much of it is in fact intelligent life, just like human beings. He was then sent hurtling off from the center of the Milky Way Galaxy and out past other, older galaxies in the universe, taking in all kinds of sights as his consciousness expanded along with the universe itself.

As he reached forth in this fashion, he soon reached the end of the physical universe. He found himself outside of space and time in the empty, eternal space that had existed before creation had even been conceived. Thomas referred to this realm as the "Eye of Creation." Thomas realized that this was the pre-creation space from which had erupted not only the Big Bang but the eternal substructure from which an infinite number of universes had been created. This is, in fact, something that many scientists would currently agree with!

According to many experts in quantum mechanics, there exists a high probability that don't live in a universe; we live in a multiverse. Notable physicist Michio Kaku has even gone on the record to state, "There are vibrations of different universes right here, right now. We're just not in tune with them. There are probably even other parallel universes right in our living room—this is the reality of modern physics. This is the modern interpretation of quantum theory."

Thomas was not a very religious man prior to his experience, nor was he well versed in quantum mechanics or any other form of physics. And yet he says he was shown that these incredible sounding ideas constitute the true nature of existence. Michio Kaku believes that other universes or dimensions exist; we are just not "in tune" with them, or as Dr. Alexander described it, our brain filters out these other aspects of reality while we are locked into the very narrow bandwidth of perception that humans are accustomed to operating on.

Likewise, Thomas maintains that he jumped across the universe, and from reality to reality, as easily as someone moving the dial on a radio to change the station. With the blocking filter of the human brain sloughed off, all he had to do was "tune in"—and he was there. After Thomas had his fill of these revelations, it was made clear to him that he would return to his body, come back to life, and let the world know what he had learned.

Thomas Benedict would later learn that he had already been dead for an hour and a half when he miraculously opened his eyes again. Even though he was consciously aware that he had been given another chance, Thomas still describes it as quite a shock to find himself back in his human body after taking such a mind-bending journey across the universe. As he gathered his senses, the first thing he noticed was the sound of his caretaker sobbing and crying in the next room.

She had apparently given up on him over an hour ago, and she was grieving for him as if he were a member of her own family. It was deeply touching for Thomas to hear her mourning for him, and he wished to let her know that there was no reason to be sad. The next thing he knew, he was trying to get out of bed to go to her, but then he slipped and fell right onto the floor.

His hospice nurse heard this commotion and ran back into the room. She got the shock of her life when she saw that her terminal cancer patient, whose body had been stiff and dead for over an hour, was now very much alive. Shortly thereafter Thomas was taken to be seen by his personal physician, and incredibly enough, his cancer had completely disappeared. The doctor was quick to inform him that his was a very rare case of "spontaneous remission," but somehow Thomas Benedict knew that it was much more than that.

# Chris Russell Makes God Laugh

This story demonstrates that NDEs can take all shapes and forms, from the majestic and incredible to the downright ridiculous and funny. Chris Russell took this to a whole new level when he allegedly provoked God to laughter by requesting that he be allowed to go back to Earth just so he could cash his social security check one more time! It's a funny story, but even funnier is the fact that Chris Russell remembers virtually none of it.

That's right; the Chris Russell NDE case is unique in that he was only informed of his supposed NDE after the fact. As the story goes, Chris, a Vietnam veteran and cancer patient, was in the middle of what was meant to be a lifesaving surgery when he abruptly died on the operating table. Bearing testament of the sad legacy of the Vietnam War, Chris was in the predicament he was in because of the long lingering effects of a little something called "Agent Orange," a deadly defoliant that was sprayed in the Vietnamese jungles.

It had been determined that the cancer had most likely emerged as a result of his prolonged exposure to Agent Orange all those years ago. The triggering mechanism for his carcinoma lay dormant for decades only to erupt with full force late in his life. As he rapidly deteriorated in that operating room, the medical staff tried desperately to revive him, but it all seemed for naught. Not knowing what else to do—as even the most skeptical of doctors are prone to doing when all else fails—they huddled together on the other side of the room and began to pray.

This is the next thing Chris consciously remembers. As his eyes, which had been sealed shut and lifeless moments before, inexplicably popped open, he observed his physicians praying emotionally for his recovery. The prayer was abruptly put on hold when one of the technicians noticed Chris trying to sit up on the operating table! Channeling Dr. Frankenstein, the tech screamed, "He's alive!" and the whole medical crew rushed over to his bedside. Chris Russell, meanwhile, had no idea his heart had even stopped and did not understand what the commotion was all about.

It was only when the medical team had gotten over their shock and disbelief that Chris was made aware of what had actually transpired during the surgery. He was informed that he'd started talking as the doctors were cutting him open on the operating table. Alarmed at the thought that Chris's anesthesia was wearing off, the surgeons immediately stopped what they were doing, fearing that he was about to wake up.

But as they listened carefully it became clear that Chris was engaged in some kind of conversation. As the conversation progressed, they grew amazed at the subject matter and just who Chris was talking to. Apparently he was talking to none other than Jesus Christ! According to those who heard it, Chris Russell was arguing back and forth with

Jesus about how he needed to come back to Earth, and one of the immediate objects of his concern was his desire to cash his social security check!

It was shortly after this that Chris flat-lined, resulting in the medical staff's mad dash to revive him. The story sounds patently absurd, and it sounded just as ludicrous to Chris himself, since he had no recollection of it occurring in the first place. He maintains that when one of the staff informed him of these odd happenings, he initially thought it was the doctor's attempt at a sick joke. He was actually offended, because he thought they were somehow making fun of him.

But the medical team all verified that the event did indeed occur, and the doctor promised that he would put transcripts of the odd conversation (as much as the medical team could remember) into his medical records. This was not the only verification that Chris would receive in regard to his forgotten NDE, however, because he just so happened to have a friend whom he described as a "psychic" or "prophet of God." When he visited her place of business, before hearing a word about the incident, she readily informed him of what had happened.

She claimed to have seen a vision of the whole thing. She contends that as Chris left his body he began to scream that he was "sorry if he had hurt anyone" during his time on Earth. The psychic says that it was this heartfelt cry of repentance that got him such divine attention. She claims that Jesus and the angels came right over to see what the commotion was all about. And Chris, not quite comprehending who he was standing in front of, began rambling as he was accustomed to doing.

Not holding anything back, Chris voiced his misgivings about the whole death thing by unabashedly announcing that he had just been approved for social security and wouldn't have to work anymore, and how bummed he was that he wouldn't get the chance to enjoy it! According to this supposed clairvoyant's interpretation, Jesus was so amused by the man's antics that he immediately agreed to heal him.

According to the psychic, Christ stepped right over and laid hands on Chris, and that was when he spontaneously revived and opened his eyes in the operating room. Chris's friend told him that he had been given several more years of life in order to fulfill his purpose here on this plane. Chris was excited to hear that he had a purpose in life—and a lot more to look forward to than a check from the Social Security Administration!

After his near-death experience Chris was a markedly changed man, and although he'd imagined himself spending his twilight years in deep relaxation, he began to volunteer many hours as a counselor at his local VA. He even went back to school, and as one of the oldest members of his class, he obtained an advanced degree in social work! You really can't make this stuff up, and this is certainly one of the most unique NDEs on record.

# Leonard Makes the Best of His NDE

Leonard Smith flat-lined in the hospital only to find himself outside of the physical form that the ER staff had been frantically working upon. From his new vantage point he could see with perfect clarity, seemingly from multiple locations all at once. Like a movie scene cutting to different cameras, he could see from above his dead body, from below it, from the left and right, and even from behind the hospital bed upon which his corpse rested.

He could even take control of any one of these "astral cameras" and zoom in on that specific aspect of the scenery, seeing it in even greater detail. As Leonard describes it, he was "traveling at the speed of thought." As soon as he thought about seeing something, as fast as he could think that thought, he was there. Even though his body was laid out dead or dying on a gurney, Leonard was so fascinated by his newfound abilities he couldn't help but explore them further.

At this point he simply walked through the wall of the operating room. The thought that he could walk through solid matter was thrilling to say the least, and like a child who is given a new toy, he began testing the limits of the phenomenon. He went halfway through structures and even walked through people who passed him by! He was quite happy to do a little bit of haunting mischief even while his body was getting more and more lifeless just a few rooms away.

Leonard eventually found himself in the hospital lobby, where several people were in various forms of repose in the early morning hours. He began dancing around these people, even putting his hand right through one of them, to see if he could elicit a response, but they were all completely unaware that he was there. While he was playing around like this, though, he noticed the next aspect of his newly acquired abilities: He realized that he could actually hear all of the thoughts of every person he encountered.

At first he thought he was just hearing their normal speaking voice, but then he looked at the face of one man in the lobby. His lips were sealed shut, his mouth wasn't moving, and yet Leonard could hear words coming forth from this individual as if he were speaking. He was actually hearing the man's thoughts! He tested this ability by going around the room and focusing on each and every person in the lobby.

It soon became clear that all he had to do was concentrate on someone in order to eavesdrop on the innermost secrets of their mind. It was like tuning into a radio station, except that he could hear thoughts instead of mindless pop songs. He soon grew bored with this, however, and instead found himself thinking of his mother. To his immense delight, as soon as he thought of her, he was standing right there in front of her inside her living room on the other side of town!

Leonard realized that time and space had no hold over him whatsoever. After briefly visiting with his mom, he decided that he wanted to look around a little more—okay, much more. He immediately transported himself right off the planet and began to explore the entire universe! He traveled across the cosmos, witnessing stars being born and planets being formed. In the middle of this cosmic voyage, he was suddenly surprised by a black hole that appeared out of nowhere and sucked him inside.

He was amazed to find other living entities inside this dark tunnel, and as he put it, "some were human, but some were not." He found that he could communicate telepathically with them, and together they came to the realization that they were "all dead." After communing with these fellow dead souls, Leonard's attention was drawn to a bright light at the end of the tunnel. As in so many other stories of NDEs, Leonard immediately felt the pull of this light.

Apparently the powers that be, thinking that Leonard had haunted the universe long enough, had this light suck him out of the tunnel he was in and toward the outer realm in which the light resided, outside of the physical universe. Physicists are often asked what is on the other side of a black hole—well, according to Leonard (and many other NDE accounts), it's the afterlife!

If such testimony is to be believed, these exit doors of the universe are apparently floating out there in deep space all the time. When Leonard made his own exit out of this reality, he left created space behind and found himself in the heart of a being of living, intense light. Like so many others, this light instantly filled him up with peace, love and happiness. And not only that; he felt that the light was somehow healing and correcting him, scanning him for problems and then ironing out any flaws it discovered.

The light then began a discussion with Leonard. He asked it, "Are you God?" The light being then shot back a line that could have been taken out of the Bible as it answered in the affirmative, "Yes, I am the light!" It was an echo of the words of Christ when he told his disciples, "I am the way, the truth, and the light." Leonard says that this being, the creator of the entire universe, actually knew him on a very intimate level. The being of light knew every detail of his life from beginning to end.

It was on the heels of this realization that something interesting happened. Leonard was able to shake off a kind of cosmic amnesia, and he suddenly remembered all sorts of "lost knowledge" that he didn't know he had! Leonard suddenly knew all the secrets of the universe, and he maintains that he didn't learn them, he just suddenly remembered them. This carries forward the concept Dr. Alexander introduced when he claimed that our consciousness is capable of realizing and understanding a whole lot more once it is free from the "filtering effect" of being cosmically live-streamed through a human brain.

After this revelation, Leonard's NDE went forward with the standard "life review" that so many others have reported. Leonard and the being of light (God) observed his life from beginning to end. He was able to witness every pivotal event, re-experiencing his emotions at the time and also the emotions of others. As is so often reported, during this review Leonard was able to see every altercation he'd had in life through the eyes of others. He was able to feel precisely how he made other people feel in any given situation.

From his omniscient viewpoint, Leonard was able to feel the pain he had caused others. If he got in a fist fight in high school and punched a classmate in the head, he viscerally felt the blow himself as he relieved the experience from the other side! Later, thinking back in wonder on this event, Leonard stated, "I dare not imagine what Adolf Hitler underwent (in his life review) feeling the pain of millions."

Leonard says that this review was meant to be a learning experience in which he could see things from every perspective and see the good that he did as well as the bad. He found out that every action had a consequence and nothing was forgotten. He even saw a few misdeeds he had thought he'd gotten away with. For example, he saw a scene of himself stealing candy from a store when he was eight years old. At the time, he'd thought, "Wow! I got away with it! Nobody saw me!"

Leonard now realized that although the shopkeeper had not seen him, his crime had nevertheless been recorded into the infinite ledger of the universe. But even though all of his flaws and vices were on open display during this review, Leonard maintains that he never once felt judged by his creator. He only felt unconditional love that would not change, regardless of what he had done while he was alive. According to Leonard, not only was God not mad at him, he even used a very human-like humor to help him feel at ease.

During the theft scene, for example, the entity surprised him by remarking, "Hmm! You thought you were going to get away with that, huh?" Rather than condemning him, the comment struck Leonard as absurdly funny and he couldn't help but laugh about it. It was thus made clear that although the life review serves a purpose as a learning tool, it is not something to beat yourself up over. As Leonard remarked, "Life on Earth is a big drama when you experience it, but it should not be taken too seriously!"

Repeating a theme that many NDErs have repeated before, Leonard states that life on Earth is just a phase. As important as we make things out to be, even the most dramatic or traumatic of events are dwarfed and meaningless in comparison to eternity. There is an old Christian hymn, "Turn Your Eyes Upon Jesus," that seems to encapsulate this theme of the afterlife quite nicely. Its refrain states that Heaven will make the things of this world "grow strangely dim."

Many NDErs assert the truth in this statement. After going to the light, they all seem to feel that the afterlife has become more real than so-called "real life." As if they are waking up from a dream, everything that was so desperately important to them back on Earth becomes rather meaningless in comparison. And as for the great knowledge that Leonard regained upon journeying into the afterlife—what happened to all those universal secrets he spontaneously remembered?

Well, as in so many other cases, those incredible secrets were conveniently forgotten upon his return to life as we know it. Once his heart began beating again and his consciousness was beamed back from the great beyond to his physical body, his human brain managed to filter out most of those details. But one thing he couldn't forget was the concept that death is merely a transition, and although the temporary human hardware that we use on this planet may break down, the core of who we are goes on.

According to Leonard, he learned that we are all eternal and will exist in some form for all eternity. Not only that, he maintains that our lives did not begin at birth; we have always existed. Again bringing up the concept of the brain as a filtering device, Leonard claims that when we are born we go through a kind of amnesia in which we forget who we really are. It is only when our Earthly form dies that that information can be reclaimed.

He maintains that this amnesia is imposed so that our testing period here on Earth can be more effective. It is important in this process that we are brought here on a clean slate. But once the filter of the brain is switched off, we see and remember things as they really are. Leonard eventually returned to his body, and his consciousness was once again live-streamed from afar through the filtering mechanism of his brain, but even so, he will never look at this life, and what we consider to be our reality, quite the same, ever again.

# Steve Learned to Love Everyone

Steve Jones was not exactly a hateful person before his NDE, but he had become very cynical. He was a young man who worked a dead-end job in retail, making just enough money to survive. Due to his daily hardships he had become a bit worn down by life, and he found himself becoming a bit numb and disconnected from those around him. He lived by the motto "If they don't bother me, I won't bother them." Most of the time, when it came to his fellow man, Steve preferred not to bother at all.

On the day his paranoid schizophrenic brother barged into his room and stabbed him in the chest, as he lay on his bed bleeding, the only words his caustic mind could produce were, "I can't believe you just stabbed me." But as blood began to spray forth from his grievous wound, the reality of the situation became clear, and he realized that he was going to die. His mom and dad, hearing the commotion, rushed into the room and managed to restrain Steve's brother long enough for Steve to escape as he clutched his chest trying to stem the blood flow.

He didn't make it very far, however, and the next thing he knew the white tiles of the kitchen floor were rushing up to greet him as he collapsed. Fortunately his sister had dialed 911, and within just a few minutes paramedics were on the scene rushing Steve out the door and into a waiting ambulance. But he had already lost a lot of blood, so much that the EMTs were surprised that he was still alive. How his heart could continue to beat with such little blood was a mystery to them.

Steve remembers one paramedic repeatedly asking him, "Are you still with us?" as if he fully expected Steve to drop dead at any moment. But Steve was struggling to stay alive, and knowing that if he let himself slip unconscious, he probably wouldn't wake up, he vigorously fought the strong urge to sleep. He knew that if he passed out he would stop breathing and death wouldn't be far away. Once Steve was wheeled into the emergency room, there was a frenzy of activity all around him. The medical personnel were struggling just as much as he was to keep him breathing.

But their combined struggle was not quite enough. Soon Steve did slip into unconsciousness, and shortly thereafter he stopped breathing and his heart finally gave up its laborious struggle to keep beating. Steve was a complete flat-line on the monitors that the doctors had been scrutinizing with nervous anticipation. The drama of the ER now reached its climax with the attending medical staff screaming "Code Blue! Code Blue!" This was a clear indication that they were losing their patient—but Steve didn't have a care in the world.

He contends that at this point he didn't quite know that he was dead; on the contrary, he almost seemed to have forgotten that he'd ever been alive in the first place! According to Steve, it was just like he'd gone back to where he was supposed to be. And where was that? Steve describes ending up in the deep, dark, black void that so many

NDErs have described. But for Steve, this was a place filled with all of his faults. He believed that the darkness that surrounded him was made of his mistakes and failings.

However, he stresses that he did not feel condemned. Steve maintains that condemnation and judgment was not the purpose of this realm. Rather, it was a place of healing and acceptance in which these flaws of his personality were sorted out and addressed in order to facilitate the healing that he needed. He referred to it as a kind of immersive "group therapy" in the afterlife. During the whole process, he felt nothing but unconditional love.

Not only that, he felt unconditional love for everyone and everything else! He felt that he loved the entire universe—its pitfalls and flaws included—unconditionally. Even getting stabbed in the chest didn't change that; in this realm, unconditional love just seemed natural. You could love your own murderer without question. The love experienced here was unconditional in the broadest sense. During this cosmic love-fest, however, Steve began to feel as if something was missing. He felt that someone else should be there with him.

At first it seemed like he and the darkness were the only things in existence, stretching out for all eternity. But as he contemplated the emptiness further, he finally began to perceive the light. It appeared as a mere pinprick in the distance at first, but as he focused on it, and thought about it, the light began to move rapidly forward until a giant, brilliantly lit orb was right in front of him. Steve remained in the presence of this light, not saying a word, just soaking up its tremendous energy, for an incredibly long period of time.

He insists that while he was out of his body time ceased to exist, so even though just a few minutes may have passed from the vantage point of those who were frantically working to revive his physical body on Earth, in this celestial/spirit realm it felt as if millions of years went by while he stood in the face of this being of light. And as strange as it may seem to those of us on this side of reality, Steve was perfectly content to lap up the warmth and energy that this being of light radiated forth for untold eons.

Meanwhile, back on Earth, there were those who desperately wanted Steve to make a return appearance in our world. In a last-ditch effort to revive him, a surgeon busted open his rib cage and massaged his exposed heart with his bare hands until the organ began to beat once again. As soon as his heart started beating, Steve was abruptly pulled out of his audience with the being of light. He felt his spirit plummet back down to Earth and into his body in what he describes as a tremendously traumatic experience.

He felt as if his expanded consciousness, which had traveled the cosmos, was suddenly being forcefully crammed back into the limited confines of his body as someone would cram pickles into a mayonnaise jar. As per the usual NDE narrative, upon entering his body and perceiving again through the filter of the human brain, all of his profound experiences were instantly switched off.

Steve was deeply saddened to find himself ripped out of the afterlife. He felt as if "the gates of heaven had been slammed" right in his face. After his stint in the afterlife, Steve would spend the next six months in rehab just to get his body in good enough shape to be released from the hospital. His brother was arrested and eventually placed permanently in a mental institution.

Steve says he feels sorrier for his brother than for himself, and if he could, he would have him released. He has done a full 180 from his previous cynical attitude, his time on the other side having taught him to love unconditionally no matter what. His NDE may have begun when his heart stopped in the physical world, but it was the treatment he received on the other side that served to heal his cold-hearted nature.

# Alon Anava's Near-Death Conversion in a Taxi Cab

Alon Anava was born in the Holy Land, but up until he was 28 years old, this Israeli was anything but religious. He grew his hair out, had tattoos and piercings, and partied like a rock star. And this was indeed what he was doing in New York City on the night he died. At the party he was attending someone was passing around a bong and handed it to Alon. No stranger to this method of getting high, Alon figured it was just the typical marijuana that was standard fare at such gatherings, so without much hesitation he took a hit.

But immediately after inhaling the drug he felt strange, and he knew that he was in trouble; Alon, a veteran drug user, instantly knew something wasn't right. He felt incredibly sick in a way he never had before, and he told his girlfriend (who had accompanied him for the night) that he needed to leave the party. She called a taxi for them, and they piled into the car to go home. But in the backseat, Alon's condition went from bad to worse. He intuitively realized that he was about to die right there in the backseat of that taxi cab.

His lungs were seizing up on him and every breath was a struggle. Feeling like he was about to pass out, he opened up the window to get some air—but as he looked out, he realized that everything was somehow frozen in place. As if someone had hit the pause button on a film, time had stopped outside of his cab. People were frozen in mid-stride and birds in mid-flight. Everything was on pause, and Along again got the unmistakable feeling that "this is it" and he was about to die.

He was struck with incredible sorrow as he looked out at this frozen landscape of lost opportunity. He felt that his whole life until that point had been a complete waste. The second he came to this conclusion, it was as if the freeze frame had been released. The world continued as normal, and Alon collapsed and slumped over his girlfriend's lap as his spirit left his body. The next thing he knew he was in an empty void of complete silence.

Alon was intrigued by this silence. He insists that he had never heard such a perfect silence in all his life. We hear sound all around us on Earth; even when we think we are alone and in a quiet place, there is always a distant sound from somewhere—a car driving by, the wind rustling through a tree—there is always some underlying sound. But according to Alon, here there was no sound whatsoever, just perfect, still silence. In fact, the only thing that he could perceive at all in this empty void was his own thoughts.

Alon still seemed to have his identity, and as his memories came back, he began to consider what had led up to his arrival in this strange place. He began to ask: What happened? Where am I? To his amazement, something communicated back to him—but not through an external voice. The entity communicated by grabbing his own thoughts and forming them into words to answer his question. It told him, "You have died. This is your death."

Alon was then compelled to look down, and through the void he could now see inside of the cab he had collapsed in. Through the car's roof, he could see his dead body still slumped over his girlfriend's lap in the backseat. The sight caused Alon to think to himself in disgust, "What? This is it? This is how I die?" He had expected to live to be 90 years old and die gracefully among his grandchildren; he had never imagined he would die slumped over in a New York City taxi cab from a bad reaction to illicit drugs.

Alon was completely horrified at how things were turning out, but then things get even weirder. He dove down toward his dead body, but instead of going back into it, his spirit transported itself into his girlfriend's body! Bizarrely locked inside his girlfriend's mortal shell, he began to see a slideshow of her entire life flash before his eyes! Life reviews are a common aspect of near-death experiences, but it seems exceptionally odd that Alon managed to review someone else's life!

However, this is what he claims actually happened to him. He maintains that as soon as he got sucked into his girlfriend's body he could see all the important events of her life and how they all led up to the current moment in time. He could feel how freaked out and scared she was at having her boyfriend drop dead on her lap. After this, Alon left his girlfriend's point of reference and propelled himself into the future. Here he could see his parents and how upset they were to hear of his death. He could see them crying and grieving over his demise.

At this point Alon realized that his soul was free to go just about anywhere in space and time. Unburdened by a physical body that limits human perception, his consciousness was now completely free to move without restriction. If he thought of a place he wanted to go, he was there, moving at the speed of the very thought itself. He chose to go back to hovering above the taxi that held his lifeless body, following high above as if magnetically drawn to his own corpse.

He followed the car as it went over a bridge, but something strange happened as it emerged on the other side. Suddenly it was like Alon's celestial eyes were opened, and he could see what appeared to be bits of coded words interwoven into the fabric of reality. He could see this code everywhere, and Alon maintains that it functioned as computer code. He was looking at the very programming that holds our reality together, and it was in everything. If such things are to be believed, it puts a whole new spin on the biblical account of God "speaking" creation into existence. Was Alon viewing the very coded word that God spoke?

Meanwhile, the car was still traveling through New York with Alon's spirit following high above as if he were a balloon on a long string tied to the taxi. His perception remained virtually omniscient while he tagged along in this fashion. He recalls at one point looking over toward a building they were passing and being able to see every single person inside and feel exactly what they were each going through at that moment in time.

He experienced a boy crying in one room, a couple arguing in another, and several other instances in which he could instantly connect with multiple people. It was while he was observing the tenants of this apartment building that he felt something grab hold of him and jerk him completely out of the frame of reference he was in. He was no longer in physical reality tailing the taxi cab that held his dead body. Instead, he emerged in a strange place of complete darkness where he immediately felt something like a crushing weight on top of him.

He then becomes aware of a funnel-shaped opening underneath him, filled with what appeared to be rapidly rotating razor blades. He felt that something was attempting to push him through this funnel. The thought filled Alon with immense fear, and he struggled with all his might against the crushing force that was threatening to shove him through.

Besides the crushing pain, Alon was terrified by the complete fear and uncertainty about where he was being taken and what would happen to him. He began to scream to God for help. He says it seemed like he was screaming and struggling like this for a million years (time was much different here), yet he heard no response. He continued to be shoved into this funnel-like blender as he was slowly ripped to pieces.

But he continued his pleas to God for help, and after what seemed like an eternity had passed, he perceived a small dot of light in the distance. Like so many other NDErs, Alon began to focus on this light. It grew larger and larger, until that small dot of light now filled his entire vision. It was right in front of him now, and the former ball of light now manifested as a large triangle. Alon perceived that it was the creator himself behind this triangle.

Alon wasn't afraid of this being, but he didn't quite get the feeling of universal love that others have experienced. He was mostly just amazed that the most important entity in the universe would come to have an audience with him. He felt that if he could just reach out and touch this being of light he would be completely saved from the predicament he was in. At that moment he was hurled toward this light, and the second he made contact, like so many others have described, he was inundated with all the secrets of the universe.

He was given the answers to all his questions in one big cosmic data dump of information. Now he understood everything. Being fed this eternal wisdom of the universe struck him as an "indescribable pleasure". Suddenly, everything made sense, as if all the puzzle pieces had been put together and he could finally see the big picture. Alon insists that human beings only see one piece of this cosmic puzzle, but he was finally seeing the puzzle in its entirety.

But as nice as all of this was, Alon still felt somehow outside of this cosmic plan. As his doubts creep back in, he heard a voice tell him, "I'm very sorry, but you did not choose to be with us, so you must go." Immediately after hearing this, Alon was ripped out of this universal center of knowledge and sent hurtling back down into darkness. He found himself inside a vast room in front of millions of people who were all staring at him.

He became aware that these people knew every bad action he had ever committed in his life, and he felt completely mortified and embarrassed in their presence. The room then transformed into a courthouse just like you would find on Earth, and Alon realized that after everything he had already been through, he was now on trial. It was here that Alon finally had his own personal life review. He had to relive everything he'd done while he was alive on Earth from beginning to end, and he saw all of his mistakes in crystal clarity.

Not only did he see the sins he'd committed as they affected him; he saw how they had affected others. According to Alon, for every sin or error of judgment in his life, he had created a blemish that seeped through the entire spiritual world, ruining the experience for others. He described it as someone putting up a priceless and beautiful painting in an art museum only to have a vandal toss black paint over it. Not only has the vandal done something wrong, he has also ruined the experience for everyone else.

So it was that this celestial courtroom was attempting to make Alon take responsibility for his actions that had so disrupted the spiritual ecosystem. He was informed that he was being torn apart in the blender-like funnel in order to cut away the diseased parts of his being that were corrupted by sin. But then the celestial judge and jury that had been raised on Alon's behalf came up with a deal for him.

They told him that he had two choices: He could go back to the soul blender and finish his purging process; or he could return to his body so he could make amends and correct the problems he was creating in the spiritual world by living a good and decent life back on Earth. Alon chose the latter.

He claims that he was so happy he felt as if he were shaking hands with God. The second the deal was made, his eyes popped open in the back of that taxi. And he hasn't looked back since. Alon is now an ordained rabbi, teaching others how to make the best of their lives while they are on this plane of existence. Alon is a completely changed man, and having cast away the destructive behavior of his past, he is determined to live out his life to its fullest potential.

# Sarah's Observations of the Afterlife

Sarah Johnson's NDE story began like many others: She was involved in a bad car accident and thrown onto the pavement, and her spirit left her broken and lifeless body. This is a common backdrop for many near-death experiences, but almost immediately after Sarah's death, things began to go far off the typical path.

Shortly after leaving her body, she found herself immersed in complete darkness. She then became aware of a small pinprick of light in the distance. So far this is still fairly familiar NDE territory, but this particular tunnel of light came bearing a surprise gift. As Sarah felt herself being pulled closer to this point of light, she perceived a hideous figure standing in the middle of it.

To her horror, coming through this portal was an eight-foot-tall black creature with huge fangs protruding from its mouth. This fearsome being was surrounded by flames, and there was a strange humming sound that seemed to emanate from it. Its dagger-like teeth were bared in aggression, and Sarah instinctively knew that the creature was coming for her with the worst of intentions.

She found herself paralyzed by fear of the entity as it rapidly advanced upon her. Forgetting all about the crash, the possibility of being dead, and all the other trappings of a near-death experience, Sarah began to wonder to herself, "What is this? Am I on another planet or something? Is this another dimension?" But as the creature came closer, all that she could really think about was how scared she was.

In the void that she was in there was nowhere to run to get away from the monstrosity, so she did her best to face it instead. She clenched her fists, gritted her teeth, locked her knees (insofar as her spirit *had* knees, anyway) and braced herself for impact. Just as she closed her eyes she felt the creature pass right through her spirit-form. Just like in a ghost movie, she was apparently intangible and things—including horrid toothy creatures—could pass right through her.

But even though the entity could not hurt her physically, she felt incredibly violated by the intrusion. As the creature passed she was disgusted to hear its evil laughter echoing all the way down the tunnel of light. Not exactly a pleasant way to begin a near-death experience, to say the least! After this exchange, she continued her progress down the tunnel toward the light at the end—but as she progressed she was disconcerted to find more of the same menacing creatures awaiting her.

She says that these entities all looked identical, basically like 8-foot-tall demons, except that they were different colors (monsters have to color-coordinate, right?). Each one of these creatures did the same thing as the first, gleefully passing through her while laughing as if it was the funniest thing in the world. It didn't hurt her, and there were no lasting effects from the intrusions, but there seemed to be no real rhyme or reason why it happened.

Regardless of the purpose behind it, these creatures just seemed to enjoy the thrill of rushing through and scaring the daylights out of an unwary human as she crossed over to the other side! After enduring these pranks for a while, Sarah came to the entrance of the lit-up part of the tunnel. From this section on, she could see that the tunnel was made up of storm clouds, spinning and writhing in concert with the frenetic energy of the dreamscape in which she was immersed.

Looking further down the path, she could see that the tunnel dropped slightly and branched off to the right. She continued her progression down the tunnel and saw that there were open doorways on the sides of the tunnel walls. Through each doorway she could see a different state of existence for souls in the afterlife. She then happened to look down at herself and realized that she no longer had a recognizable physical body; she seemed to be simply a nondescript glowing ball of blue light.

She looked back up the tunnel and saw several other floating blue lights just like herself. Two more blue orbs then appeared behind her, and she was surprised to have them gently push or nudge her forward in the tunnel. This is another common theme with near-death experiences: The NDEr is pushed by another, in order to facilitate, or move forward, the next part of the experience.

Sarah then found herself floating further down the tunnel. She began to look at some of the doorways along the walls. She says that she couldn't see through all of them—some were blacked out and obscured—but through others she could see all kinds of strange and thought-provoking landscapes. One doorway in particular sent a chill up and down her spine: It opened onto what was unmistakably the traditional hell featured in so many Earthly religions.

Through this door she could clearly see people in all manner of suffering, being tortured in unspeakable ways by bizarre monsters, seemingly sentient animals, and even the classic variety of demons with pitchforks. The landscape was absolutely apocalyptic, like the molten floor of a volcano, and most disgusting of all, there were rivers of blood and human excrement flowing across the landscape!

Basically, if it was horrid and disgusting, this place had it! Sarah found herself voyeuristically intrigued by what she saw, and she couldn't help but stop and observe the happenings beyond this doorway. Then a sudden sucking sensation propelled her right through it! She was terrified, but it soon became clear that nothing would harm her here. As she floated above the suffering, she was literally "above the fray." It was immediately made known that she was merely there to observe; she was not meant to be involved in the pain and suffering of this hellish landscape.

When she looked back toward the door she saw that it was wide open, and that it could be seen from any point of reference in that hellish realm. Even though it was a small portal in the tunnel from whence she had come, from the ground below, the doorway seemed to be huge and expansive. It was a giant landmark on the horizon, easily visible. And yet the tortured souls so desperate to get out couldn't seem to see it, even though it was right in front of them.

Sarah realized that these people were so absorbed and consumed with their own personal suffering that they couldn't even take the time to look up and see that an exit to their pain and misery was right there in front of them all along! Feeling sorry for these hapless sufferers, she went back through the door and into the hall, leaving that painful place behind for good. She then decided to go further down the tunnel to see what she could see.

As she peered through the doorways, the next environment that stood out to her was one of a vast desert landscape. People who seemed to be suffering from severe depression were mindlessly walking through this empty desert, completely immersed in their sadness and sorrow, not paying any attention whatsoever to the people around them. It is interesting to note that this plane of existence has been described before by other NDErs.

One of the more famous among them is Angie Fennimore, a wife and mother who attempted suicide and ended up in a very similar place. Fennimore claims that she was walking through a desert landscape with all kinds of sad and distraught people who were mumbling and muttering to themselves incessantly about their own personal pain and sorrow. They seemed completely incapable of doing anything but wallowing in their own misery.

They were so self-absorbed they couldn't even look up and see the people walking right next to them. In Fennimore's NDE, she was told that this was a resting place for suicidal souls who were completely consumed by grief and anguish in the end of their lives. Due to this negative emotional baggage with which they entered the afterlife, they were being forced to quite literally "walk it off" until they could function normally.

Sarah quickly grew tired of this way station of the despondent. She gave it a brief once-over, but did not even bother to go through the door before continuing down the tunnel. Finally, she came upon a door through which she saw a scene of absolute beauty. This place was the complete opposite of the sadness she had seen before, a place of beauty and profound joy. It had all of the typical trappings of a heavenly paradise.

There were majestic forests, green grass, rippling springs, rivers of pure blue water, and warm and loving rays of light illuminating the whole environment. Sarah felt compelled to go into this realm, but as she willed her little body of light through this door, something happened. She felt like there was some barrier preventing her from going forward. Then she heard a voice coming from inside. It informed her in a matter-of-fact manner, "You do not have the information to enter this world."

She didn't have the right information to enter into paradise? It came as a sad realization for Sarah that she was being turned away from this veritable garden of Eden. She was so determined to get in that she ignored the voice and attempted to force her way through the door. There was to be no breaking through this heaven's gate, though; every time she pushed on the barrier, she was knocked backward like a luminous Ping-Pong ball, back into the tunnel.

Realizing that she would not be allowed to enter, she decided to go down the part of the tunnel that branched to the right and descended down lower than the rest of the maze. At the end of this part of the tunnel she found herself in front of a giant yellow-and-white orb. She felt immediately drawn to this entity, and as soon as she entered into its presence she felt an "indescribable feeling of joy" and a kind of perfect harmony with all of creation. She felt as though everything was right, and in its place, that everything served a purpose, everything was going as planned, and there was absolutely nothing wrong with anything.

The universe, all of creation, was perfect and without blemish. This was the serenity that she experienced in this light. Immersed in this loving feeling, she felt free to announce herself to this entity and basically told it, "Hey! I'm here!" As funny as it may sound, the being responded with the enthusiastic affirmative of "Great!" Sarah then gave herself to the light completely and merged with it. She explained later that, rather than just *feeling* joy, she literally *became* joy.

Peace, love and happiness was all that she knew. But incredibly enough, after a while, she began to grow a little bored with pure happiness and peace! She told the being of light as much, informing it, "Hey! I'm leaving!" The being responded with its characteristic affirmative, "Great!" as she wandered away from it and back down the tunnel.

According to Sarah, the great takeaway from all this was that whether she was around this light force or not, it would still project peace and tranquility, and she could always come back to it when she was ready.

It was like an eternal soul-charging station where she could always give her celestial batteries a boost of happiness when she needed to.

Continuing forward on her journey, Sarah reached the end of the tunnel and found a doorway that interested her greatly. Looking out of this doorway, she could see the entire physical universe. This was a window into outer space, and she realized that now that she was out of her physical body she could roam the entire cosmos as a disembodied sprit!

The idea thrilled her to no end. She liked the idea of being able to float forever and discover new things as a cosmic tourist floating through the universe for all eternity. But as she was preparing to jump through this doorway, another orb of light appeared next to her and began to question her decision, reminding her that she still had family to look after on the other side. She began to think of her son, and how hard it would be for him to grow up without her, and began to have second thoughts about the whole thing.

She heard voices coming through the door she was about to enter, and they all informed her that if she did decide to go through, she would not be able to come back. She would be effectively stuck floating through space for the rest of eternity! It was then that she finally made the decision she hadn't quite known that she had to make—she decided to return to her body.

Even though it felt like she had been in that tunnel of light forever, Sarah found herself back in her body shortly after the accident had occurred. She came to in a hospital bed with all kinds of tubes and monitoring equipment attached to her. She had a respirator down her throat since she couldn't breathe out of her smashed lungs, and her entire body was broken and battered.

But even so, she felt filled with incredible power. This was apparently an after-effect of her NDE, and after a few moments of being back in her body it wore off. As it did, the incredible pain of her shattered physical form made itself known and she came back to the physical reality of what was occurring after her accident.

Many have found her tale just a bit too hard to believe, but Sarah insists to this day that it is the absolute truth. This inquisitive woman was taking notes during her trip to the afterlife, and she knows what she saw. Nothing is going to convince her otherwise.

# Naomi's Journey to Beyond

Naomi had collapsed in bed in utter exhaustion thinking that she just needed a little bit of rest, but when she woke up at four in the morning unable to catch her breath and with a horrible pressure on her chest, she knew that she was having a heart attack. After being rushed to the hospital in full-blown cardiac arrest, she found herself floating up out of her body and toward the ceiling of the emergency room that held her dying form.

Looking down from her vantage point near the ceiling, she could see the ER personnel desperately attempting to revive her. She saw them pounding on her chest and shoving tubes down her throat. She saw her own form limp and lifeless as they worked on her, with her arm dangling off the side rail of the gurney.

They say you can find humor in anything, and as the ER staff performed CPR, Naomi was struck by how funny her body looked as they pressed down on her. She found herself laughing at the way her dangling arm bounced around like a mannequin's appendage whenever they applied pressure. Amusement aside, Naomi was amazed that even though her corpse was lying there dead and flopping around like a lifeless dummy, she was completely free of pain and very much alive.

In fact, she had never felt so alive in her life. Like many NDErs, Naomi reports that she felt as though all of her senses—her entire consciousness—had been greatly expanded when she left her body. It was in this new awareness that she noticed a bright light emerging from her left side. As soon as she turned to look at it, the light expanded out toward her, as if in recognition that she was there waiting for it to present itself.

This light normally would have been completely blinding in its intensity, but since Naomi was now observing it with spiritual eyes rather than physical ones, she was able to withstand the bright searing light. As she stared at the light she realized that it was somehow alive, and as the light drew nearer she was filled with the most incredible sensations of love, peace, and happiness, more powerful than she had ever known.

She was immediately drawn to this presence, wanting more of the powerful emotions that it engendered. But it wasn't only strong emotion that the entity evoked; it also produced a strange sense of familiarity. Somehow, as Naomi neared the light, she had the feeling that she was going home. Not only that, she had the odd sensation that the world she was leaving behind was not entirely real in the first place. It was as if she were waking up from a dream and reality itself was just a figment of her imagination! This is another quite common thread for NDErs: Many have this inescapable feeling that the afterlife is somehow "more real" than normal, everyday life down here on this planet.

Enveloped in this hyper state of love and her newfound awareness, Naomi urged herself to move completely into the light. The next thing she knew, she began a kind of life review in which she saw important moments of her life from the present moving backwards, like a tape rewinding all the way to the beginning. Incredibly, this life review actually ended with her seeing herself in her mother's womb! She claims that she could feel the sensations she felt as an unborn child, feeling the warmth of being inside her mother and experiencing vibrations of sound as her mom talked and laughed.

This aspect of Naomi's experience does seem a little unusual when compared to other NDE stories. For one thing, in the vast majority of cases the life review begins with the person as a small child and then flashes forward all the way to the person's last moments on Earth. For some reason Naomi's life review went backwards from the present all the way to before she was born.

After this odd experience, Naomi felt herself being pulled into a deep black void of nothingness. She felt as if her sense of awareness, her very identity, was beginning to fade away altogether. Her attention was then drawn toward a nearby presence. She couldn't quite see them in the darkness yet, but she distinctly felt that someone was there with her in that deep dark void of nothingness. She attempted to focus on this outside form of consciousness waiting in the darkness with her, and she suddenly became aware that this figure was her mother. Her mother had passed away years before, and Naomi had missed her dearly.

Both Naomi and her mom spontaneously coalesced back into human form for the encounter, and the two approached each other out of the darkness and exchanged a loving hug, overjoyed to be in one another's presence once again. After this heartwarming moment with her mom, Naomi became aware of even more familiar presences emerging out of the ether. These were mostly people that she had known while she was alive.

There were also some other figures there as well. Naomi didn't actually know who they were, but she had the distinct impression that they were angels or some sort of ministering spirits working to help facilitate her encounter with people from her past. The next thing Naomi knew, her mother was sternly informing her that she needed to go back to her old life, and that there were people on Earth who still needed her among the living.

This made Naomi very frustrated, and as if she were living one of her childhood arguments with her mother back on Earth, at one point she started yelling, "I don't care! It's my life! I should have a say-so!" The only thing the two needed was an agitated Naomi slamming a cosmic door in her mom's face! But wading through all of the arguments, her mom informed her, "It's not that you don't get to choose. Part of you, in fact, is choosing and participating in this decision."

Like moms do, Naomi's mother reminded her child that she shouldn't take the easy route. "It would be easy for you to choose to stay here, but you know on a level you can't quite comprehend just now that there is more you need to experience and learn from your family relationships—and more they need to learn from you. When choosing is not an act of escape but an act of completion, then you will stay."

Her mom was trying to remind her that she was on a mission while on the Earth. When she still had work to do among the living, she couldn't just take the easy way out and give up. Fortunately, she didn't need much more prodding from her mother. Before her mom had to resort to "But what would the angels think?" Naomi relented, took her mother's piece of wisdom, and agreed to go back. As soon as she made this pact with her mother, she was back in the operating room where physicians were feverishly working on her to save her life.

Yet she wasn't back inside her body yet; she was still outside of herself, watching the proceedings as a silent observer. Then a voice she felt reverberating from inside her broke in to predict that her forlorn physical form was about to have another heart attack, announcing, "Here it comes. Get ready for it." The next thing she knew her body was convulsing on the table as the doctors took countermeasures to bring her back to life.

She watched them as they slid a board under her back, and she remembered the doctor suddenly yelling at the technicians, "Whoa! Whoa! My stuff! My stuff!" This utterance would be verified by the amazed physician when Naomi came to. The doctor confirmed that he yelled those words because one of his assistants had nearly knocked his medical tools to the floor by being too careless with the board.

The doctor, who was a natural skeptic about such things as NDEs, became a true believer when Naomi told him she'd heard him say these words. He knew that there was no other logical explanation for it. The doctor knew that she had not only been unconscious; she had been dead on the table! The machines Naomi was hooked to clearly showed that her heart had stopped. That was why the techs were scrambling to put the board underneath her, because the flat surface of a board is used to help with CPR.

It's a rather innocuous comment to be used to prove life after death, but he knew there was no possible way she could have heard him yell "Whoa! My stuff! My stuff!" while she was dead on that table! Stories like this seem to prove that there must be much more to our consciousness and human identity than a three-pound hunk of grey matter can convey. And even cutting-edge science is beginning to back this up.

The concept of "quantum entanglement," in which molecules have been found to react and respond at mind-boggling distances, suggests that information can be sent and received at the quantum level in ways that we do not completely understand. If a molecule can communicate to another molecule on the other side of the universe, demonstrating Einstein's "spooky action at a distance," then perhaps our consciousness is being beamed from eternity to the radio receiver called the human brain in much the same manner.

Exploring this radio analogy further, just think about what it means to turn on a radio and listen to music. Where does that music originate from? As much as we like to think that it comes from our radio speaker, and our favorite performers are jumping around, live in our boom box, it does not. Our radio is merely receiving a signal from a radio station, making it seem that that particular bundle of radio waves resides in our radio itself. And what happens when we turn that radio off? The signal goes back to its source. The signal isn't dead, it has just returned where it came from.

And when we turn the body off? When the body/brain dies, isn't the signal of human consciousness simply returning from whence it came? Is this why so many NDErs feel as if they have returned "home"? It seems that a whole new understanding of consciousness—and maybe even what it means to be "alive" in the first place—is on the horizon.

# Ray Kinman Sees the Face of God

In the late 1960s, Ray and Chris were the best of friends. Their families knew each other well, and they both attended Catholic school together. The two were inseparable, and they were together on the day of Ray's remarkable NDE. School had just let out, and they were standing on the sidewalk talking and killing time, waiting for their ride home. In the course of their small talk, Chris mentioned to Ray that he had just started judo lessons after school and had learned how to toss an opponent over his shoulder.

Intrigued, the adventurous Ray requested a demonstration of this feat. He wanted his buddy to give him a good toss or two so he could see it in practice. Chris gladly complied and began to hoist Ray up into the air, but instead of tossing him over his shoulder as planned, the still inexperienced Chris misjudged his aim and accidentally slammed his friend into the ground head first. As Ray's head crashed into the pavement, he immediately knew he was in trouble.

He felt pain from the tip of his skull on down his spine and into the toes of his feet. The traumatic brain injury caused his brain to misfire, and he began to choke on his own tongue as his body struggled to breathe. Soon he started to suffocate, and the lack of oxygen his prompted his body to rapidly race toward death. The next thing Ray could perceive was being in a state of nothingness—and in Ray's case, this void didn't even have darkness. According to him it was as if he were suspended over a blank page of nothing, as if nothing existed at all.

Ray still didn't understand that he was dead—obviously this is not a thought that would come easily to a 9-year-old—and so he assumed that he was going crazy. He had heard stories of people losing their minds and hallucinating and seeing things that didn't make sense, and he thought that must be what was happening to him as well. But he figured that there wasn't anything he could do about it, so he decided to let his perceived insanity run its course.

At this point, Ray simply "let go" and stopped struggling with the state of existence that he was in. And as soon as he let go, his frantic thoughts began to calm. This calm was then superseded by a strong feeling of contentment, followed by a growing happiness, which soon became sheer bliss. Ray wasn't sure where these great feelings of joy were coming from, but as he looked over his left shoulder and saw a bright pinpoint of light suddenly emerge from the blank void, he had the feeling that this light just might have a little something to do with it!

He describes this light as being "brighter than the sun," and—as seems to be quite common in NDEs—he was rapidly pulled toward it as if by magnetism. As he drew nearer he realized the light was actually a tunnel or portal, an opening in the blank realm of nothingness, and as he reached the threshold of this opening he was sucked through it and "spit out" the other side.

On the other side of this cosmic rabbit hole he found himself standing on a giant dais and looking up at huge golden columns that seemed to be rising up to infinity. He felt that he was standing before some sort of great gateway. A human-looking entity then stepped out from behind one of the columns and told him, "I want to show you something." Ray claims that the split second this creature told him this, he felt an explosion of information, as if it were being downloaded directly into his soul. Like so many others have reported, Ray felt as if all the secrets of the universe, the answer to every question he had ever had, were immediately known and made clear.

Back on Earth, meanwhile, his classmates had summoned adults to the scene, and they were desperately trying to revive him. They looked on his lifeless body with sadness and fear as they waited for an ambulance to arrive.

But beyond the barrier of life and death, Ray was very much alive, and he was being made to understand all there was to know about all of creation and existence itself. After this cosmic data dump, the entity before him said, "Now I want to show you God." The next thing he knew, he was staring at what appeared to be an entire galaxy spinning in space. He came to believe that this network of stars was somehow the face of God.

He could see all the points of light that made up this galaxy, and he felt that all of them radiated the deepest and most powerful love. His awestruck fascination was interrupted when the mysterious guide next to him informed him that it wasn't "his time" yet and he had to "go back." Very similar to Steve's experience of being crammed into a "mayonnaise jar," Ray felt horrible discomfort as his consciousness was being shoved back into his body.

He even said it felt "gross." After his majestic experience, being shoved back into his flesh, felt like he was being shoved into a pair of "crusty old socks." He remembers that when he came to, he was crying. First responders thought that the tears were from the pain of his injury, but Ray knew that his grief was out of despair at leaving the heavenly realm of knowledge and bliss that he had experienced in the afterlife.

Shortly after his recovery, Ray told his mother just what had happened to him. Although she did not understand exactly what her son was telling her, she wanted to be supportive, so she referred him to the parish priest, hoping that he could provide some answers. The priest wasn't having any of it, however, and since Ray's NDE did not include an obvious appearance of Jesus, he rejected it outright as a deception of the devil.

Ray was devastated at this unbelief from someone he saw as a spiritual advisor. The experience caused him to bottle up and hide his NDE over the next several years. He is now a middle-aged man, and only just recently has he come to grips with what happened to him on the sidewalk outside of his school all those years ago.

# Choo Nam Thomas and Her Tour of the Afterlife

So far in this book we have discussed people who've had encounters in the afterlife through what we term a near-death experience. But there are those who have claimed to have had the same exact experience without having to die! Choo Nam Thomas is one of these claimants. Choo Nam Thomas—who finally did pass away in 2013— was a Korean American who was born in Japan to a family she claims knew almost nothing about Christianity. During her life in the United States, however, Choo Nam became a devout believer.

For many years she maintained a laser focus on her faith and prayed constantly to be closer to God. According to Choo Nam, after all of her prayers and supplication, God decided to grant her request. She claims that in 1996 she was woken up at four in the morning to find herself being visited by none other than Jesus himself—who immediately spirited her off to heaven, apparently just to show her around!

Many, of course, scoffed at this story and were quick to write Choo Nam off as either a fraudulent attention seeker or mentally deranged. However, she never changed her description of her heavenly encounter. It allegedly began on January 19, 1996, when Choo Nam woke up at three in the morning with her entire body shaking. She claims it was like every muscle of her body was on fire, trembling and shaking.

This phenomenon went on for an entire hour as she lay there in bed. Then she heard an odd popping sound that prompted her to turn over and look in that direction. To her amazement, there at the side of her bed, she perceived an entity dressed all in white. It was just standing there, watching her. She was not at all afraid of this being; on the contrary, she could feel the love radiating forth from the figure, and she immediately realized that the visitor was none other than Jesus Christ.

At this realization she began to cry uncontrollably, but the being intervened to stop her flow of tears. "My daughter, Choo Nam, I am your Lord, and I want to talk to you. You have been my special daughter for a long time." As soon as she heard the being's voice, the force of the words hit her like a wave of energy and her convulsive shaking increased until her entire body was vibrating.

The being departed soon thereafter, and Choo Nam fell into a deep sleep. For those tempted write off this experience as just a particularly vivid dream, it would have to be a recurring dream, because for the next several weeks, Christ visited Choo Nam in the exact same fashion every single night. The tremendous shaking at the onset of the vision actually become so pronounced that Choo Nam's husband, Roger, volunteered to sleep in the guest room!

This went on until February, when Choo Nam claims that Christ returned and told her with a sense of urgency, "Daughter, I must show you some things." Choo Nam began to experience the same shaking sensation, except with much more force. This shaking soon became an intense vibration all over her body, as if every molecule of her being were rapidly vibrating. The vibration was actually so intense that she felt as though she were about to be ripped apart at the seams, into a billion pieces flying in all directions.

At this point she became very frightened, screaming and flailing her arms in the air as she wondered what was happening to her. (Even though he was in the guest room, Roger must have been a sound sleeper to have missed all this!) The vibration then increased to a climax and she felt herself pop right out of her body. She was now in spirit form, and she was transported directly to heaven. When she emerged into the afterlife she was in a new body that was much younger and healthier; she was in perfect shape.

She found herself walking with Christ along a vast, empty beach. They then traveled from the beach to somewhere further inland, where she saw a large hill that seemed to be "alive with foliage" and had a long zigzag path from its bottom to its summit. Passing by this hill, Choo Nam noticed other land and water forms, including a river which had the "most crystal clear" water she had ever seen.

The two followed this river until they reached the entrance of what Choo Nam refers to as a "shiny tunnel" situated across the river. They walked through this tunnel before emerging on the other side in front of a huge pearl-white gate (the "pearly gates," perhaps?) just outside of a large and majestic white building. Choo Nam and her divine guide walked through the gate and continued on to the building. Upon entering the building they walked down a long hallway that took them to a large room.

The walls of the room were composed of glowing shiny stones that provided a beautifully ambient effect. As they stepped into this room Choo Nam felt a weight on her head and realized that she was suddenly wearing an ornate crown of gold. She looked up to find Jesus sitting on a throne in the center of the room. After this visionary experience she found herself instantly transported back to her bed, wide awake and staring up at the ceiling.

This event was followed by another on February 24th, in which she woke up shaking with the voice of Christ telling her simply, "We are going to heaven." She was once again taken through a huge tunnel that was "bright and shiny" and transported to heaven. Interestingly, while she was in transit, the thought occurred to Choo Nam that this must be what "people who have near-death experiences report."

As she emerged on the other side, she saw the same large white gate she had seen before. There were beautiful flowers growing on each side of this heavenly border wall, and she again felt overwhelmed with joy that Jesus would give her a "personal tour of the afterlife." She says that Christ then led her to the giant white building that was just inside the gates. As they walked up the steps, Choo Nam stared in wonder at the giant double doors that led inside the structure.

These doors were framed with gold and had stunning stained glass paneling on each side. Choo Nam and Jesus walked through these doors and found themselves standing on a floor of white marble. She was then led into what she says was the "throne room of God." At this point the details of Choo Nam's story become a little hazy. She doesn't directly describe what she perceived God to look like; she just describes seeing a figure on a "glistening golden throne" and that "beams of radiant glory" emanated from where he sat.

Incredibly enough, before she could gain a direct audience with the creator, Choo Nam claims that an angel directed her to a dressing room in order to make herself a little bit more presentable for the event! This angel took her to the side and led her to what she described as a "powder room" where she found all the trappings of an extravagant dressing room like you might find on Earth.

There was a full-length mirror that covered the wall. There were velvet chairs in front of it, so people could sit in comfort while they fixed themselves up! There was also a giant walk-in closet with many gowns, robes, and even crowns to choose from. It is this aspect of Choo Nam's story that strikes many as being utterly ridiculous, but she is certainly not the first to have bizarre encounters in the afterlife, and she will certainly not be the last.

Celebrated NDE aficionado Colton Burpo of *Heaven is For Real* fame, for example, made the odd claim that everyone in heaven carried a sword at all times just in case the realm were ever threatened with invasion! Many Christians who were otherwise fans of Colton's story were taken aback by this strange statement; they weren't entirely sure why heaven would need a citizens' militia!

Many of the odd aspects of an NDE, whether they are random dressing rooms or the sword-toting faithful, can seem hard to swallow. But besides the nearly identical general mechanics of how they operate—life review, intense vibration, transportation through a tunnel, feelings of indescribable joy, and so forth—each NDE seems to have some aspects that manifest simply for the benefit of the individual experiencing it.

This has led some to believe that the afterlife will be whatever we want it to be. If you want there to be a dressing room in heaven, there will be a dressing room in heaven. Heck, if you want there to be a Taco Bell in heaven, there will be a Taco Bell in heaven! Supporters of this theory are quick to point out that those who have the rarer but much more dramatic hellish NDEs tend to be people who have died in a particularly negative fashion (such as suicide) or who are consumed with a tremendous amount of guilt.

These poor souls seem to have their hellish state of mind reflected back on them. For those who promote this theory, it thus makes perfect sense that the details of the experience could vary so widely: They are custom-fit and tailor-made for those who experience them. At any rate, after Choo Nam's wardrobe change, she was wearing a fresh gown and crown and sent back out to the main room of the building she had been taken to.

Jesus was waiting for her there with a matching gown and crown just like hers. This manifestation of Christ then took her out of the throne room and back into the courtyard outside. He walked with her to another building which Choo Nam described as looking like a "medieval castle." Inside this castle, Choo Nam took in even more aesthetic sights of beauty such as "elegant furniture" and ornately laid carpet.

Not to be too critical of Choo Nam's NDE, but up to this point, her story seems incredibly superficial. However, things would take a turn for the deep and philosophical soon enough. Choo Nam was shown some rather terrifying visions of a possible future Earth engulfed in natural disaster, war, and social chaos. She observed a scene where future earthlings ran in absolute panic from their homes in the middle of the night, some only half dressed, as if the crisis had unfolded so rapidly that they did not have time to prepare themselves.

She was then taken on a tour of hell, and similarly to some of the other accounts mentioned here, Jesus informed her that the only people who suffer in hell are those who *want* to suffer in hell. Choo Nam's vision of Christ told her that he welcomes all to heaven with open arms, but he does not force anyone to walk streets of gold if they do not want to.

Just as Sarah Johnson's NDE indicated, the denizens of hell seem to be made up of those guilty souls whose own self-loathing is so great that they wish to punish themselves for all eternity. What can we really make of Choo Nam Thomas's tour of the afterlife? Is it just wishful thinking on her part, or something more? I guess we'll just have to wait for our own tour to find out.

# Natalie Sudman and the Audience of One

Have you ever had the odd feeling that your whole life was a movie and a hidden audience was watching your every move? I'm not trying to rip off the plotline from *The Truman Show*, but this apparently is a theme that comes up in NDEs from time to time, and the case of Natalie Sudman seems to be one of them. Natalie was a civilian contractor working in Iraq at the height of George W. Bush's so-called "surge" in 2007.

She was working for the Army Corps of Engineers on a construction project, putting in busy 12-hour days surveying various landscapes, when the convoy she rode in was blown up by a roadside bomb. The day it happened was a typical day like any other, and she recalls that she was rather bored, just looking out the window, when the bomb went off. Several people were killed, and Sudman was severely injured in the blast—but according to her, the very second the bomb blew, she was transported somewhere else.

She didn't feel the blast, because in the blink of an eye she found herself not in a blown-out Humvee in Iraq but on stage in a giant stadium with thousands of white-robed figures standing around watching her. Even more peculiar was the fact that she immediately knew where she was and what she was doing. She instantly realized that her entire life had been a kind of role-play that she had been conducting for the benefit of all these other beings that had been watching her life from beginning to end.

Now, remembering her true purpose and realizing that the game of her life was over, she began to telepathically upload the information to all of the beings in attendance so that they could digest the data in full. Harkening back once again to the concept of the brain as a limiting filter, Natalie claims that once she was free of her body and in this other realm, she once again knew the big picture and who she really was. No one had to explain anything to her; she naturally understood the entire situation.

It was an odd sight for sure. There she was in this other state of consciousness, wearing a pair of U.S. military fatigues and sending a mental data dumps of her life to thousands of white-robed celestial entities—and it seemed perfectly normal to her! In fact, the whole thing seemed almost like it had been planned in advance.

In the weeks leading up to the roadside bomb attack, Natalie had had a feeling that something was about to happen. She'd even caught herself mindlessly packing her things, as if on some subconscious level she expected to be leaving soon. Her tour of Iraq was supposed to last for several more months, but due to the attack she would be leaving much sooner, and she seems to have intuitively known this on some level, well in advance.

As for the environment in which she shared her life with the beings, Natalie says that it was as if she were on a platform floating in outer space. She seemed to be in a black, velvety void, and like outer space it was dark yet faintly illuminated at the same time. It was in this otherworldly environment that Natalie found herself standing before these robed beings. She claims that the general feeling from these beings during her "data transfer" to them was one of admiration.

They seemed to admire the fact that she had been able to live a life on Earth and go through the things that humans normally go through. According to Natalie, not all spirit beings have the strength or ability to meld their consciousness to physical form and be born as a flesh-and-blood human. Natalie explains that being sent to live out a life on Earth is just one of the tasks that these beings were capable of, and some could do it, and do it quite well, but others could not.

It was as if each had a different skill set, and while some were perfectly capable of encasing their spirit in flesh and being born, for others the task would be too difficult. Natalie recalls that it was those who didn't have the strength for the "human mission" that admired her the most. However, since she was "quite good at it," it was no big deal for her at all, and so she took such admiration in stride. It would be like someone who can't play guitar looking with admiration at someone who plays with ease. It was just that some had the ability, and some did not.

According to Natalie, all of this complex metaphysical discourse happened in the blink of an eye. As many have maintained, this afterworld environment had no sense of time. She could have been there for several hours, even though only a second had passed on Earth from when the roadside bomb rocked her convoy in Iraq's desert. In this blink of a second, however, she learned quite a bit as she shared every detail of her life up to that point with her celestial "colleagues."

While she didn't exactly feel the incredibly unconditional love that so many other NDErs have described, Natalie did feel an avid interest and passion for her life from all of these beings. She doesn't describe it as them having compassion for her; rather, it was a "co-passion" in which each one of them was equally passionate about her existence on Earth and seeing the story of her life play out until the end.

These entities apparently wanted to continue watching the story of Natalie's life, however. They requested her to go back into her shattered body so they could view her full recovery and the continuation of her life on Earth. Natalie at first refused, telling them that she was tired and just wanted to move on to other things. Natalie maintains that the beings were okay with that, but still insisted that it would really help them out if she would return. She didn't have to, but they would really appreciate it if she did.

Natalie finally agreed, not because she was forced to, but simply because she wanted to help her fellow celestial beings out with an experience that apparently only she could provide for them. It was here that Natalie realized that every single human life is incredibly unique and valuable, because it creates an important learning experience for the celestial beings that vicariously experience it through those who choose to be born.

So it was for this reason, to help these beings in their learning process, that Natalie agreed to go back. And since they were so desperate for her to return, Natalie saw an opportunity to sweeten the deal for herself. She informed them that she would only go back on the condition that she remember her audience with them upon her return. Apparently, if she had not thought to strike this bargain, she would have forgotten all about her time in the "blink environment" as soon as she returned to her body, and none of us ever would have heard this bizarre little story!

After a brief discussion, the beings agreed to this arrangement, and the next thing Natalie recalls is her and two others from the assembly coming back to Earth to the scene of her death. For them, time had stopped, and the scene of her mangled body splayed out in the blown-up Humvee was frozen. This feature of Natalie's NDE is strikingly similar to that of Alon Anava, who also described an instance in which everything in the outside world was put on "pause."

As they hovered over this freeze-frame, Natalie and her colleagues began to use their "energy" to heal her body. Her blown-up body was not in good enough condition at that point to return to life on its own, so it needed some healing—but they did not want to heal it completely. Apparently wishing to follow the roadside bomb script, and not wanting anything to look too miraculous, the beings determined that Natalie needed to be injured, just not *that* injured.

Once Natalie's body was healed sufficiently according to this standard, they discussed how they should arrange the remaining injuries. She says that this is where they really had "fun." As they floated above her physical body as balls of light, they began to play with the grievous wounds! They put a hole in her side at one point, just to see how it would look. Then they put a wound in her head, but decided that brain damage would probably ruin the experiment. Then they made her lose a hand, and according to Natalie, they all thought this was "really funny." They were even laughing about what life would be like for her without a hand. Natalie is the first to admit how bizarre all this sounds, but she contends that things are just much, much different when you are out of your physical shell and experiencing the world as an observer from the outside.

It seems almost like these beings were playing with what we view as "life" as if it were some kind of goofy computer game. It makes you think of someone playing *The Sims* or some other real world simulation game where you get to create characters from scratch, putting a mustache here, an earring there. It seems that these beings were having the time of their lives rearranging their "Earth Avatar" of Natalie's broken body in the Humvee in much the same fashion.

According to Natalie Sudman, from that vantage point, tragic things (or at least, tragic to us) are just "funny." There are so many nuances to Natalie Sudman's NDE that in many ways it is one of the most complicated to explain. Perhaps this is why she named her book about the episode *Application of the Impossible*. For after her impossible gathering with these celestial entities, she did eventually jump back into her body to tell us the story—and what a story she had to tell!

# What Does It All Mean?

There are so many riveting stories of those who claim to have been to the other side that it is hard to dismiss them outright. And as you have no doubt noticed by reading all of the accounts presented in this book, there are several common threads among all of these stories. Although certain surface details may vary, the core mechanics of the experience remain the same.

It seems that almost everyone who has an NDE leaves their body and finds themselves pulled in by a brilliant tunnel of light; hence the cliché "Go toward the light!" It also seems that almost every NDEr feels an unconditional love and support from this light. Most also have what is termed a "life review," or as it is more popularly expressed, "their life flashes before their eyes."

Almost everyone who experiences this life review describes an expansion of consciousness in which they perceive their own life as an omniscient being, suddenly able to see things from all sides. They are uniformly awestruck to be able to re-experience every aspect of their life from all perspectives. They are not only aware of their own emotions; they also directly experience exactly how every other person involved was feeling during the exchange.

Imagine the husband who beats his wife being forced to feel the fear and victimization of his spouse. Likewise, imagine an abusive wife who frequently belittled and harassed her husband suddenly understanding just how bad she made him feel! These are all incredibly powerful aspects of the near-death experience, and for the most part they remain fairly universal for all NDErs.

The only thing that might vary from person to person is who or what the "bright light" represents. Sometimes it manifests as a religious figure, and sometimes it is perceived as pure cosmic energy. These surface features vary, but the core experience remains just about the same. Due to all these similarities, it is hard to outright discount the multitude of testimony heard from all over the world.

Even the biggest skeptic has to admit that *something* is happening to these people. They aren't (for the most part) making all this up! But if they aren't making it up, then what is leading to such a universally similar experience? Well, if we listen to the cold and clinical analysis of the scientific community, some explanations for the common features of NDEs have been proposed.

The part of the near-death experience that involves seeing deceased loved ones or balls of light, or even leaving the body itself, is attributed to "hypoxia." Hypoxia refers to the reduced level of oxygen in a dying brain. According to this theory, it is the lack of oxygen that causes many of the strange sights and sounds that occur in NDEs.

Oh, and what about the feeling of unconditional love and happiness that leaves so many NDErs feeling so incredibly moved? The scientific community contends that this is nothing more than the brain releasing its entire store of endorphins at the point of death, which gives the dying such a rush that they forget all pain and feel nothing but a chemically induced high of "pure happiness."

There have even been explanations proposed for the "tunnel of light." According to some, this is just a result of an excess of carbon dioxide creating a kind of "tunnel vision," which in the bright lighting of a hospital could be interpreted as a tunnel of light.

Now that we have delved into the more mundane proposals, I would like to apologize to anyone who has actually had an NDE and feels the urge to punch the computer screen at such meager attempts to explain it!

But don't worry, because there remain aspects of the near-death experience that the world of science has never been able to explain. Take for example all those cases of patients who flat-line and are pronounced dead—but who upon resuscitation several minutes later give a full report on not only what was said in the operating room, but also what was happening down the hall!

Take the case of Naomi, whose heart had stopped, whose brain activity had completely ceased, yet who remembers all that was said and done. This sort of phenomenon has never been explained, and if instead of attempting to debunk near-death experiences, science was used to prove their veracity, the whole concept of life and what we understand to be consciousness just might be turned on its head.

# Further Reading

*Near Death in the ICU*. Laurin Bellg
Written by a veteran ICU doctor, this book relates several fantastic yet well documented tales of NDE. If you are looking for compelling evidence and eyewitness accounts that are hard to discount, this book is for you!

*The Complete Idiot's Guide to Life After Death*. Diane Ahlquist
Yes, they have an "Idiot's Guide" to just about everything! Don't let the title throw you; this book actually has a lot of thought-provoking information on NDEs. Not only does it document several eye-witness accounts, it delves in depth about some of the more common mechanics of the phenomenon. A truly useful resource!

*Life after Life*. Raymond Moody
This book is truly a classic and one of the first major investigations into the field of near-death experiences. Mr. Moody's book is a tour de force and highly recommended.

*Heaven is So Real*. Choo Nam Thomas
This book is not to be confused with Colton Burpo's more famous *Heaven is For Real*. Despite the similarity in title, Choo Nam Thomas's book predates Burpo's epic by over a decade. She wrote her account in the late 1990s to document her testimony of several trips she claims to have taken to heaven and beyond.

*Proof of Heaven*. Dr. Eben Alexander
Dr. Eben Alexander had an extraordinary experience after a deadly bout of meningitis. This biographical epic is a must-read!

www.nderf.org
This is the go-to source for first-hand accounts of near-death experiences. Virtually every well-known case (and some not so well known) can be found in this massive NDE database.

# Also by Conrad Bauer

Paranormal UFO Sighting Cases that Still Mystify Non-Believers
ALIENS
CONRAD BAUER

TUNGUSKA
AN APOCALYPTIC EVENT BEYOND BELIEF
CONRAD BAUER

SHERGAR
A True Crime Story of Kidnapping, Racehorse, and Politics
CONRAD BAUER


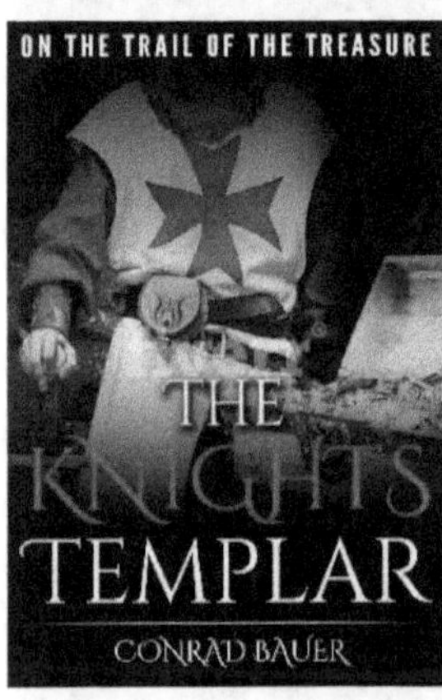

ON THE TRAIL OF THE TREASURE
THE KNIGHTS TEMPLAR
CONRAD BAUER


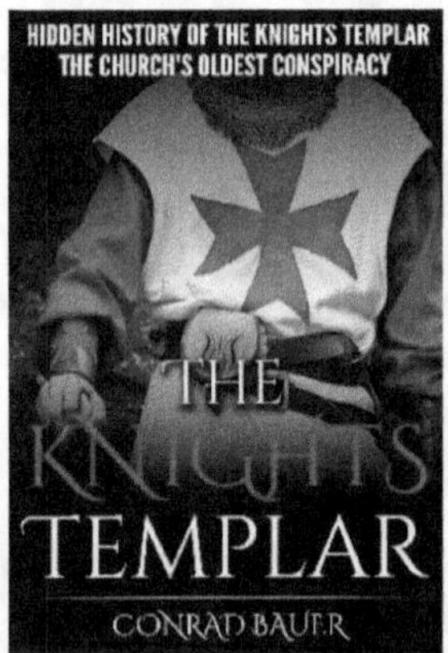

HIDDEN HISTORY OF THE KNIGHTS TEMPLAR
THE CHURCH'S OLDEST CONSPIRACY
THE KNIGHTS TEMPLAR
CONRAD BAUER


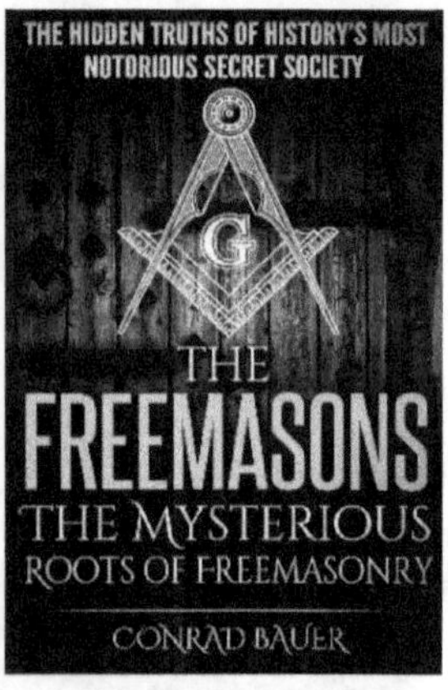

THE HIDDEN TRUTHS OF HISTORY'S MOST NOTORIOUS SECRET SOCIETY
THE FREEMASONS
THE MYSTERIOUS ROOTS OF FREEMASONRY
CONRAD BAUER

History's Most
MYSTERIOUS SECRET SOCIETIES
CONRAD BAUER

VOL. 2
THE WORLD'S STRANGEST FORGOTTEN CONSPIRACY THEORIES
CONRAD BAUER

The World's Strangest
FORGOTTEN CONSPIRACY THEORIES
CONRAD BAUER

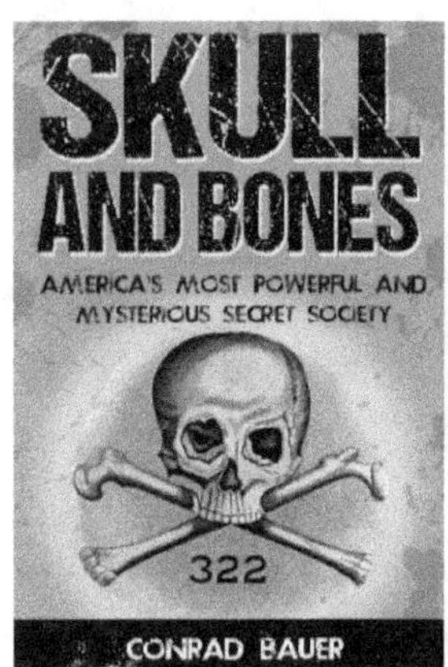

SKULL AND BONES
AMERICA'S MOST POWERFUL AND MYSTERIOUS SECRET SOCIETY
322
CONRAD BAUER

SECRET SOCIETY
The ILLUMINATI
Separating Fact from Fiction
CONRAD BAUER

HOAX, CONSPIRACY OR SECRET SOCIETY?
The Priory of SION
Conrad Bauer

CONRAD BAUER
OPUS DEI
CATHOLICISM'S SECRET SECT
SECRET SOCIETIES


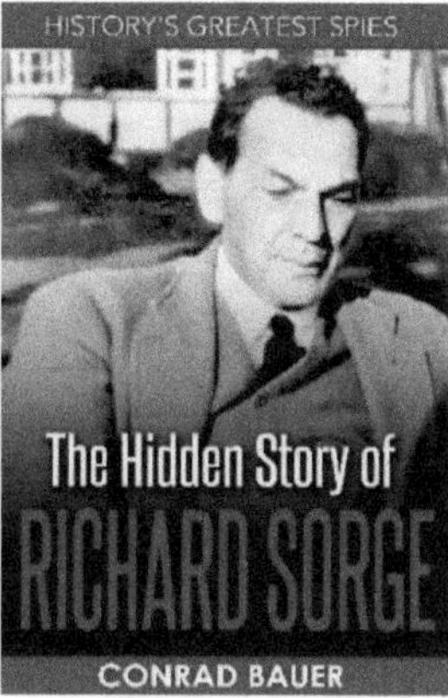

HISTORY'S GREATEST SPIES
The Hidden Story of RICHARD SORGE
CONRAD BAUER

CONQUERORS OF THE WORLD
THE VIKINGS
CONRAD BAUER

# Image Credits

Plato
"Plato-raphael" by Raphael - Unknown. Licensed under Public Domain via Wikimedia Commons -
http://commons.wikimedia.org/wiki/File:Plato-raphael.jpg#/media/File:Plato-raphael.jpg

Anecdotes de Medecine
https://archive.org/details/anecdotesdemde00dumo

Ketamine
"Home Anesthetic" by Psychonaught - Own work. Licensed under CC0 via Wikimedia Commons -
http://commons.wikimedia.org/wiki/File:Home_Anesthetic.jpg#/media/File:Home_Anesthetic.jpg

Ascent of the Blessed
"Hieronymus Bosch 013" by Hieronymus Bosch (circa 1450–1516) - art database. Licensed
under Public Domain via Wikimedia Commons -
http://commons.wikimedia.org/wiki/File:Hieronymus_Bosch_013.jpg#/media/File:Hieronymus_Bos
ch_013.jpg

Ozzie Osbourne – By F darkbladeus [Public domain], via Wikimedia Commons
https://commons.wikimedia.org/wiki/File:OzzyChangingHands02-20-2010.jpg

Jane Seymour – By Ilya Haykinson [GFDL (http://www.gnu.org/copyleft/fdl.html), CC-BY-SA-3.0
(http://creativecommons.org/licenses/by-sa/3.0/) or CC BY-SA 4.0-3.0-2.5-2.0-1.0
(https://creativecommons.org/licenses/by-sa/4.0-3.0-2.5-2.0-1.0)], via Wikimedia Commons -
https://commons.wikimedia.org/wiki/File:2009_CUN_Award_Party_Jane_Seymour_036.JPG

Sharon Stone – Georges Biard [CC BY-SA 3.0 (https://creativecommons.org/licenses/by-sa/3.0)],
via Wikimedia Commons -
https://commons.wikimedia.org/wiki/File:Sharon_Stone_Cannes_2013.jpg

Garey Busey – By Photographer JessicaPinney, portfolio (Own work) [CC BY 3.0
(http://creativecommons.org/licenses/by/3.0)], via Wikimedia Commons -
https://commons.wikimedia.org/wiki/File:CUN2008_Oscar_party_Gary_Busey.jpg

Dr. Eben Alexander Becomes a Believer -
https://upload.wikimedia.org/wikipedia/commons/4/47/Pacific_Partnership_160722-N-BB534-
451.jpg

Messiah's Near Death Encounter with Satan - http://maxpixel.freegreatpicture.com/Inferno-Hell-
Lucifer-Satan-Demon-Devil-161049

Thomas Benedict's Incredible Journey through the Life/Death Barrier - http://maxpixel.freegreatpicture.com/Heavenly-Clouds-Shadow-Blue-Light-Soul-Angel-Sky-669262

Chris Russell Makes God Laugh - https://upload.wikimedia.org/wikipedia/commons/7/7c/Cima_da_Conegliano%2C_God_the_Father.jpg

Leonard Makes the Best of His NDE - https://pxhere.com/en/photo/603005

Steve Learned to Love Everyone - https://static.pexels.com/photos/5390/sunset-hands-love-woman.jpg

Alon Anava's Near-Death Conversion in a Taxi Cab - https://pxhere.com/en/photo/1392081

Sarah's Observations of the Afterlife - https://pxhere.com/en/photo/725694

Naomi's Journey to Beyond - https://upload.wikimedia.org/wikipedia/commons/c/c3/NGC_4414_%28NASA-med%29.jpg

Ray Sees the Face of God - https://upload.wikimedia.org/wikipedia/commons/2/26/Michelangelo%27s_%22God%22%2C_from_%22the_Creation_of_Adam%22.jpg

Choo Nam Thomas and Her Tour of the Afterlife - https://c2.staticflickr.com/6/5518/11943416683_6c9eac2c5e_b.jpg

Natalie Sudman and the Audience of One - https://upload.wikimedia.org/wikipedia/commons/c/cd/Toyogeki-Movie_Toyooka002.jpg